Elizabeth Schwaiger

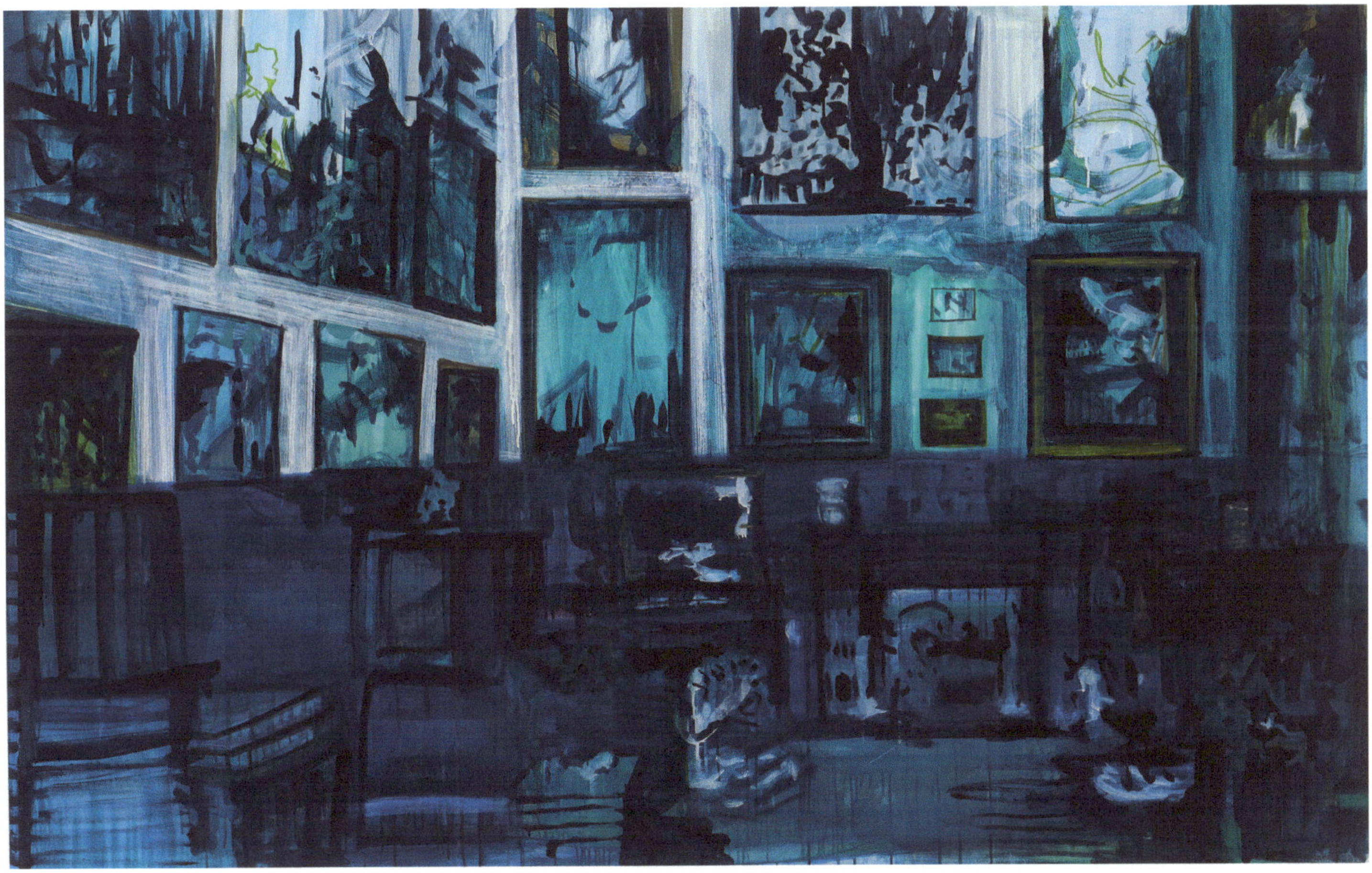

Below the Brine, 2020
Acrylic, watercolor, and ink on canvas, 48 x 76 in.
Courtesy of the artist and Jane Lombard Gallery.

Christy Rupp

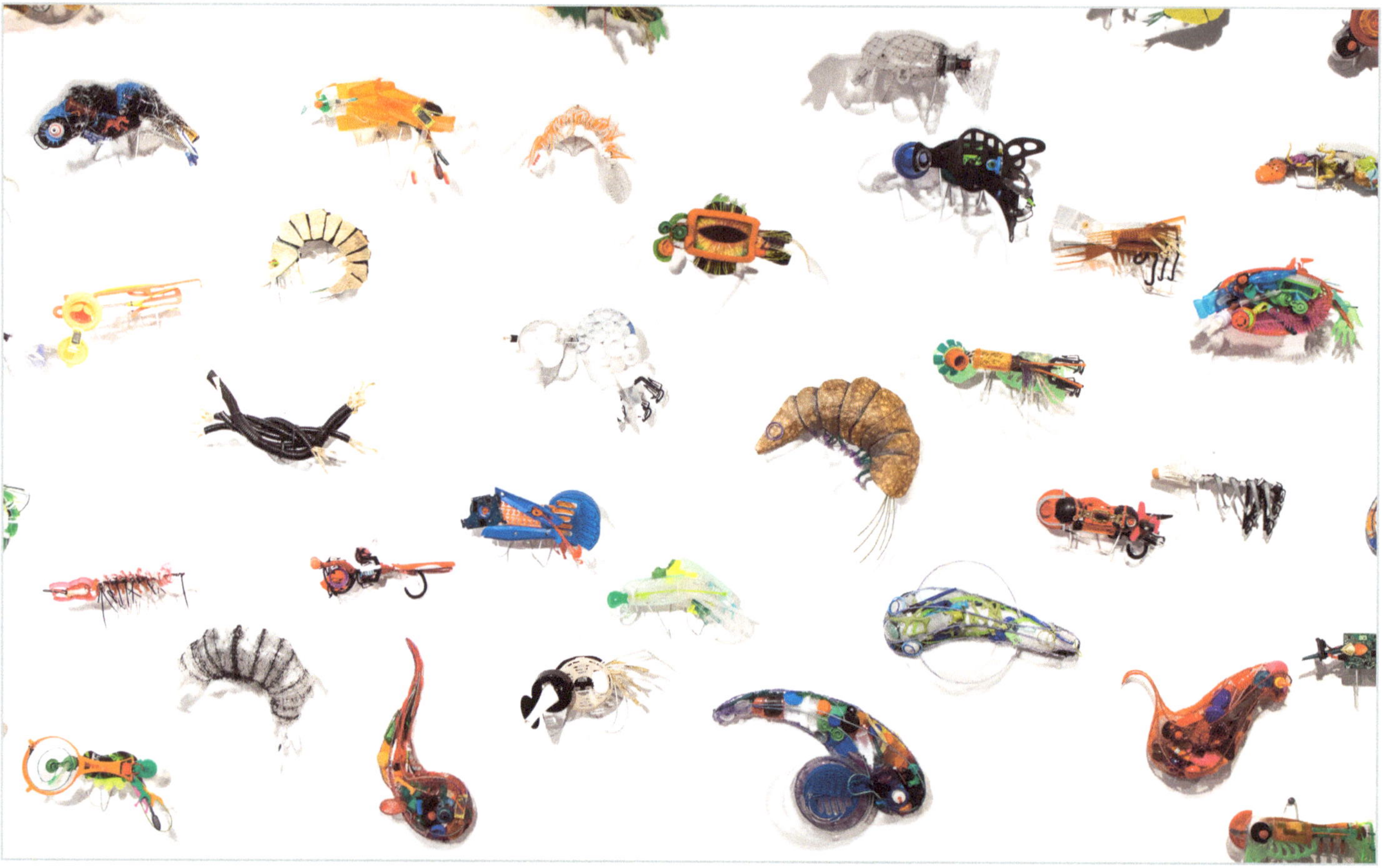

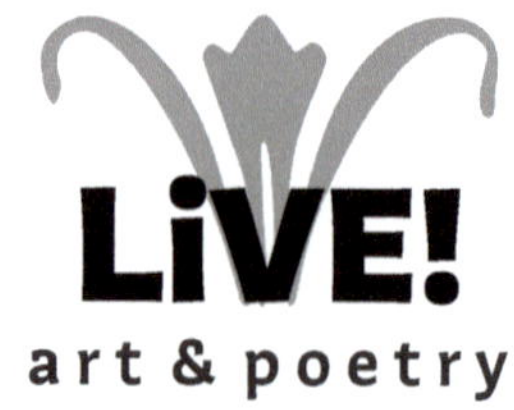

From "CHRISTY RUPP, OTHERED." Courtesy of Howl! Arts

LiVE!
art & poetry

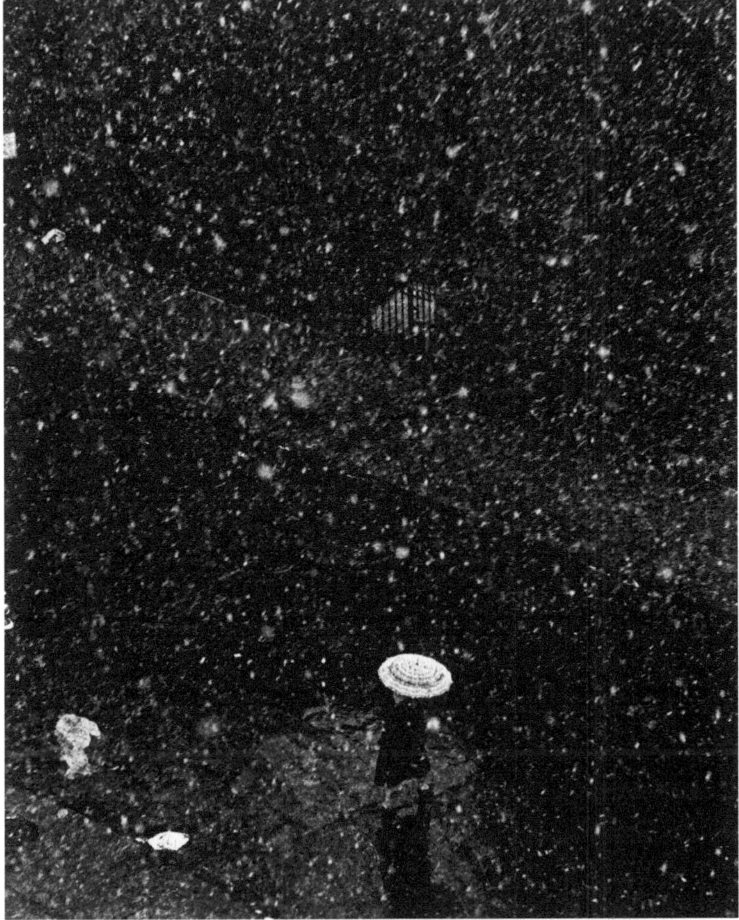

Adger Cowans, White Umbrella, 1971, Gelatin silver print, signed on verso, 16 x 24 in., edition of 5 + 2 AP. Courtesy of the artist and Bruce Silverstein Gallery, New York.

Publisher and Editor: Jeffrey Cyphers Wright
Deputy Editor: Ilka Scobie
Associate Editor: Lori Ortiz
Cover art: JCW; Design: LO
©2023 Live Mag!

Box 1215 Cooper Station, NY NY 10276

https://livemag.org
SUBSCRIBE!

№19

John Yau

From "Li Shangyin Enters Manhattan"

10. *i.m. Martin Wong (1946-1999)*

Sprayed subway sign: Living is wheezing
a horse riding through swollen veins
I press on and leave gold hand prints
In sky's blue pocket, write poems
on brick piles, I am not like the others
who drift from horny to scorn in a blink
Another slammed drunk upended
in romance's spreading muddle
The life of a Chinese cowboy
isn't all chopped duck and pinto schemes,
I have seen many boys, dead and alive
crying a thousand deaths, stripped blue in the rain
but I still love the smoky smell of a fireman's rubber coat
crispy french fries lathered in mayonnaise

What My Mother Told Me

Shanghai is an ancient seaport that no longer exists in American history books

Shanghai is found only on maps where dragons frolic in a frothy sea

Shanghai is known to hide paintings of cats licking their remaining patches of fur

Shanghai is rimmed by nuclear plants mounted on neatly stacked plates

Shanghai harbors fleets of atomic submarines rusting beneath a green tropical sun

Shanghai is a post card of iridescent mermaids lounging on artificial rocks

Shanghai is dirt piling up and obliterating whatever precedes it

Shanghai is an empty gray cargo plane leaving at dawn

Shanghai is a child's mouth filling once more with black and green snow

After I Turned 71

For Laura Mullen

I did not expect to see myself standing in the mirror

I look like someone I would never want to meet

I wonder if I have made a mistake without knowing it

I am sure the word 'disaster' does not tell the whole story

I know there is room for improvement but decide to skip over that part

I realize this passport is the last one that will be issued to me

I begin to think the joke is not only on me

I can walk in any direction and still end up in the wrong place

I stop trying to make a list of words I will never use again

I decide making sense is no longer an acceptable form of lying

I think it is prudent to let others do the counting

I often tell strangers that I start vomiting when the seasons begin changing

I agree that 'reincarnation' is a scam perpetuated by life insurance companies

I liked it when the cab driver called me 'young man' and gave him a smaller tip

Hillary Keel

Faculty Meeting, 1:30 p.m.

Late. Eyes look up. I want to explain
tardiness, the problem with the E train.
I want to explain the December light
I want them to see. Eyes look up
and to the side. A head turns, glances
sideways or diagonal, an Isosceles
triangle, or elongated rectangle.

My tardiness means nothing. Light
of December afternoon shines through
windows at top of room, above our
heads. Talk of numbers, projections
to future, a circular arc to Christmas
plans and we say, "hi" and "bye"—
a colleague grabs my arm, two or
three times, suggests we take the train
together. We're on the 6 to 28th Street
then above ground in a shop of Indian
spices and copper dishes, grains,
    and incense.

Outdoors the avenues cast rays
    of winter light.

I hike up 22nd from Park, each avenue
a new shade of sun glares through haze
with gossip of marriage and families,
the light is silver, the leaves, some still
golden, people between lunch and their
afternoon coffee, knowing the linear
trajectory in golden and silver,
the brisk air and curve of tires,
an opalescence, knowing

I am here.

Three p.m. light of children's squeals,
the haunting call of swing set
and car horn ripples the air,
crackle of back door squirrel
and light on floorboards.

Out back the Saturday night Christmas
tree stands on the wall,
    bought after drinks
and a comedy show on 23rd Street,
    after kissing
outside the Comedy Club,
    how you ran off like
an Iron Hans or a Cinderella;
    I bought that tree
afterwards on 8th Avenue,
    out of giddiness,
to remember you.

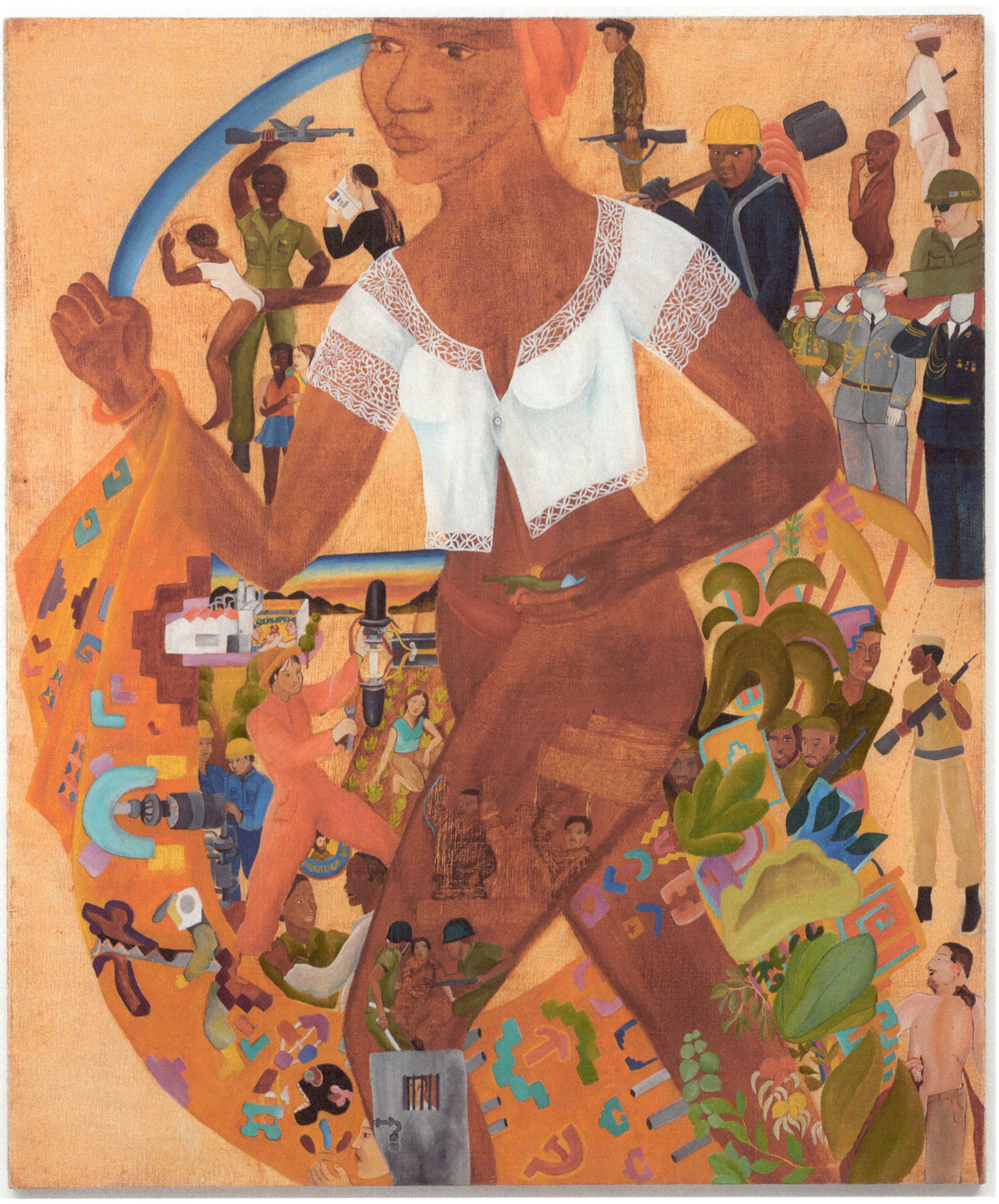

La mulata costeña de Colombia (The Mulata Costeña of Colombia) ca. 1977
Oil on canvas 47 x 39 1/4 inches (119.4 x 99.7 cm). Courtesy the artist,
Lehmann Maupin, New York, Hong Kong, Seoul, and London, and the
Solomon R. Guggenheim Museum.

Judith Simonian

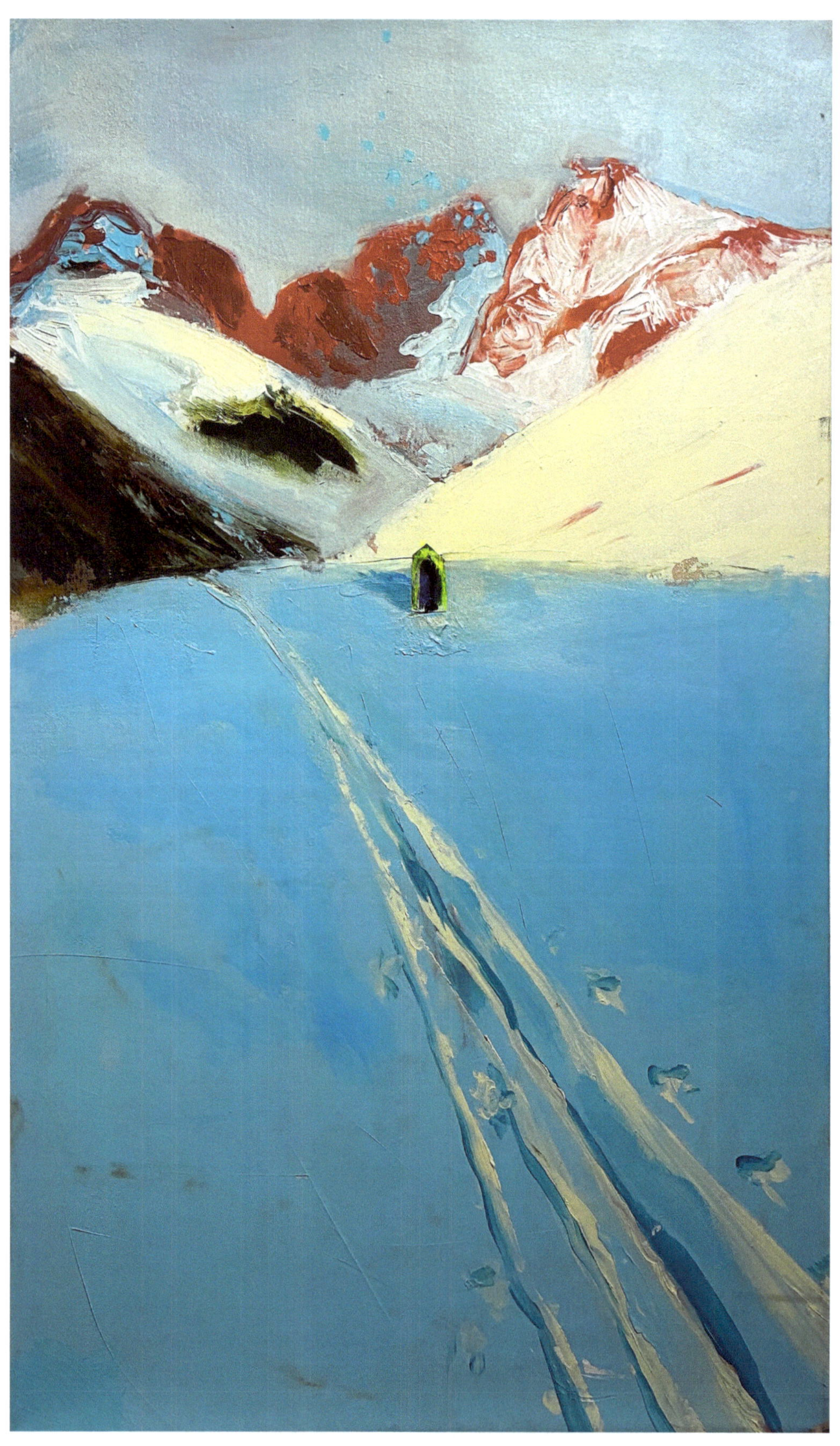

Icy Blue Trail, 2010, acrylic on canvas 28 x 18 in.
in 'PLUSH: Paintings by Judith Simonian 2010–2022 at 1 Gap Gallery

We Will Get Rich at The Funeral

We will be the liberators. We will not execute
anyone, regardless of race, creed, sexual orientation,

Or current credit score from all three major credit
rating agencies. We will fill libraries with mystic rocks

And mini-bars. We will insist that all the fathers
make amends to their daughters. No one will commit

Suicide. All Mormons will be unbaptized and turned
into Jews or atheists. Judges will set everyone free

But no one will want to be let go. Suffering is loneliness.
Sorrow grows on bones like moss on a rock.

You can look it up. Look up at the people
in the windows looking down on us. Make them take

A baby aspirin every day. Tell them you mean them no harm.
Make them fall backwards into your waiting arms.

Change of Climate

Peacocks meander through the fertile plain.
They are a royal pain. Do not try to sit one in your lap.
It would take a solitary metaphor as red as
a heart to make those birds depart.

Beggars beg beneath troubled skies,
the radio playing oracular sighs of doom.
If you let them in your room, all is lost.
It's a high cost to pay for absolutely nothing.

Let the cantos and centos gather up mementos
so no one may forget the ghost of the sea
coast, now on fire like a burning bush
of desire. The cash turned all to trash.

Jerome Rothenberg

A Reconsideration

[In Wonder at the Webb Space Telescope
& a New Image of the Deeper Universe]:

men grow old
& cry out "shit"
like children

dropping to the bottom of a well,
uncautious,
trained to fish for eels

to come up breathless
on the other side
where mothers reach out arms to hold them

"holy days" the simple man proclaims,
the shapeless wanderer
not simple only, he is open

this allows the world to look
into his eyes, to see
a depth there, like a hole in space

the farthest probe of all they call
"deep image," galaxies condensing
in the perfect poem

* "deep image": a technical term in astronomy for
photographs of the outer limits of the visible universe.

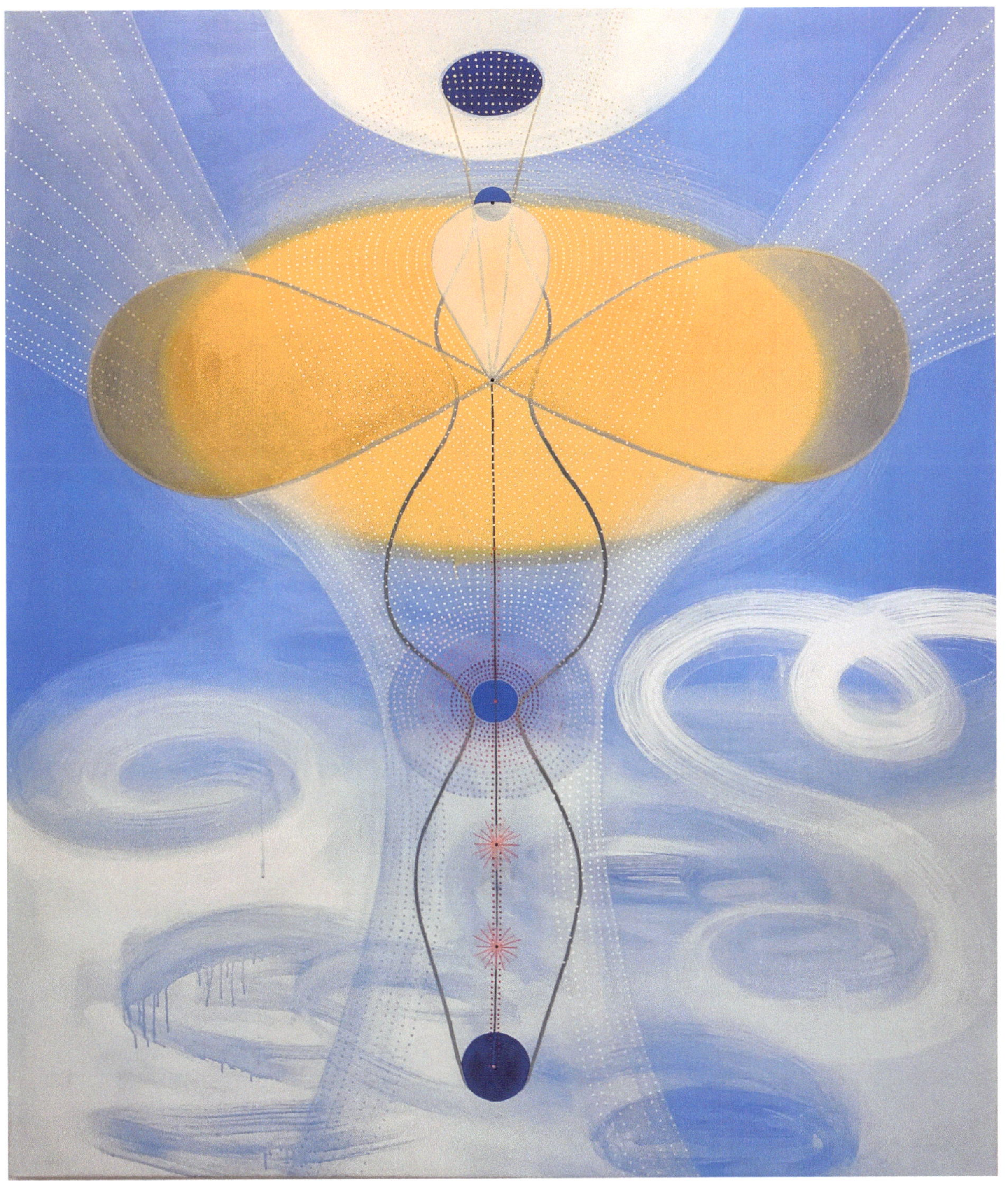

Indigo Ray Body, 2020, Flasche on canvas, 72 x 60 in.

Clive Smith

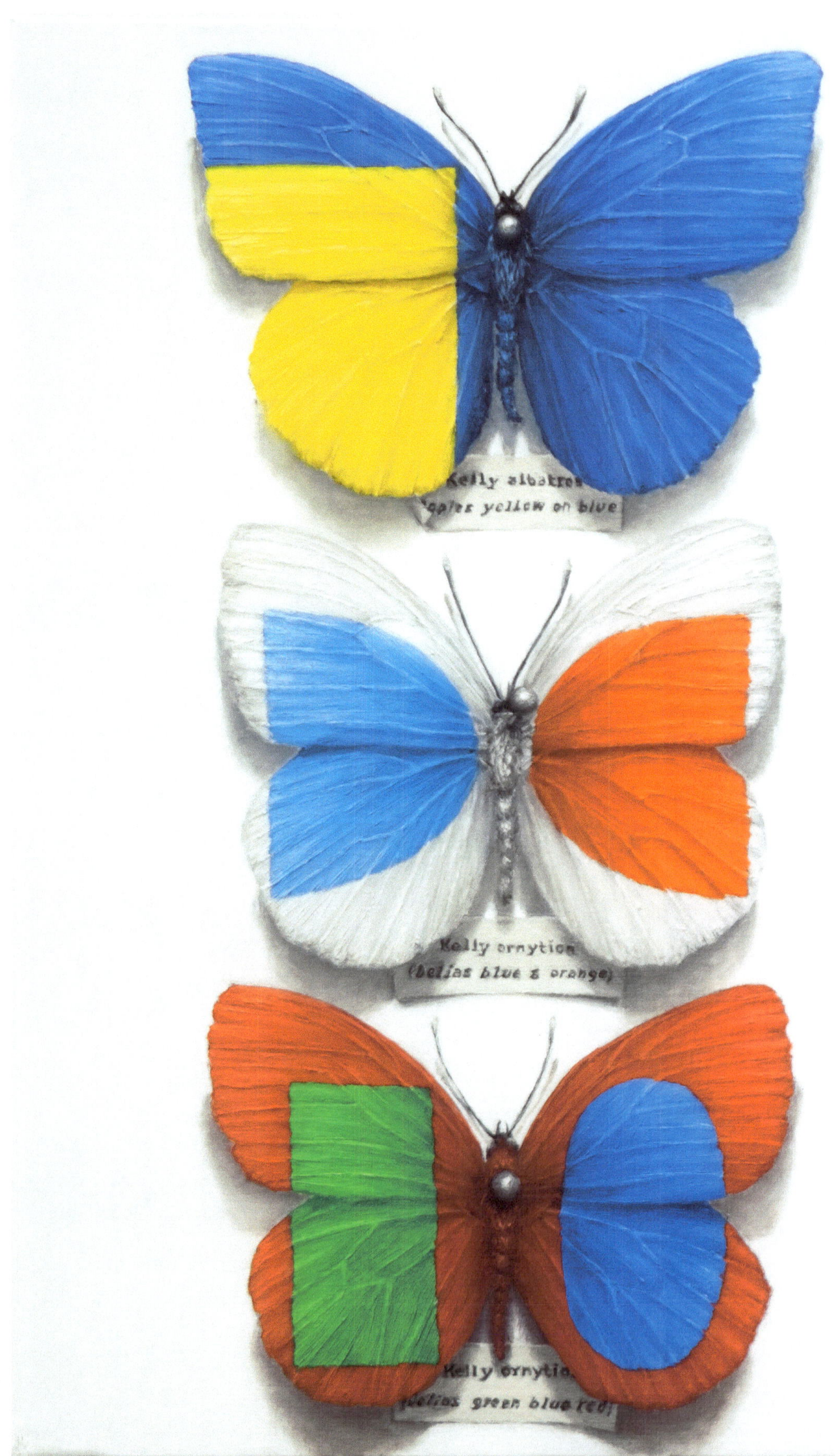

The Kelly Butterfly Collection, detail
2021
Courtesy of
Marc Straus Gallery

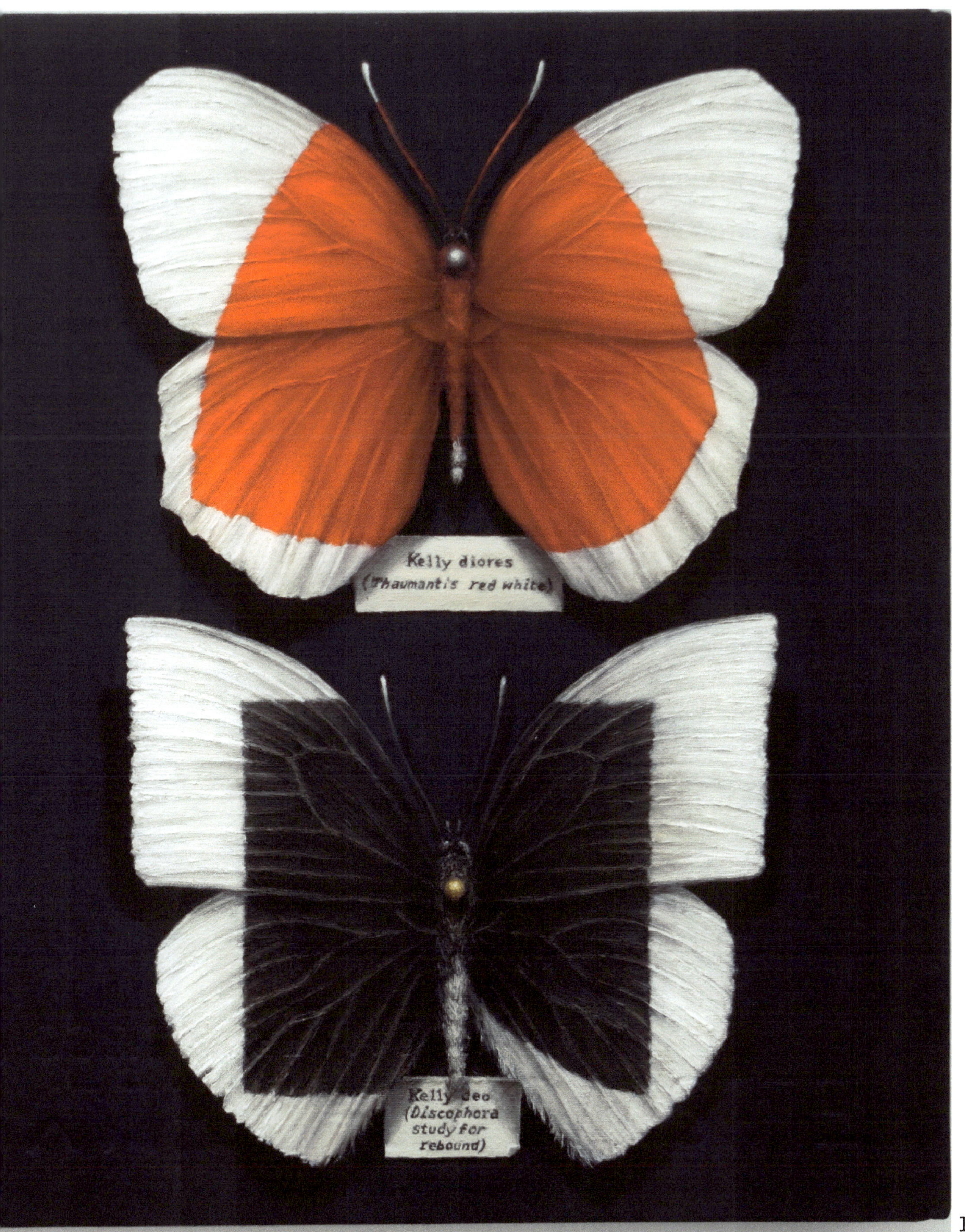
Kelly diores
(Thaumantis red white)
Kelly deo
(Discophora
study for
rebound)

Barry Wallenstein

A Kiss

In Delay, There Lies No Plenty, So Come Kiss Me
— Angela Carter

Smack me a kiss-quick
before I do it myself.
Plant your roses right here
before I abuse myself further
in front of you–or in that beveled mirror
behind you. I'd leave this ache behind
if, led by affection, the old-fashioned
getting-to-know-you, prevails.

We—if you can imagine
two small letters composing a word,
a date, a place to be in,
an hour in which to play
shy, but please,
be shy in my mouth, osculate,
and stay this way forever.

The Carnal Life

Too few were the decades
of working the blood pressure,
shuffling the rules;
misremembering each other's names.

The fist time—alone and then not—
fiercely into it, but then,
after decades,
less a thrill, less soil.

The memory bank is flush and scarlet;
the week ahead is blank and dull
but for a date with the Gonad twins,
cousins of Onan, holder of the crown jewels.

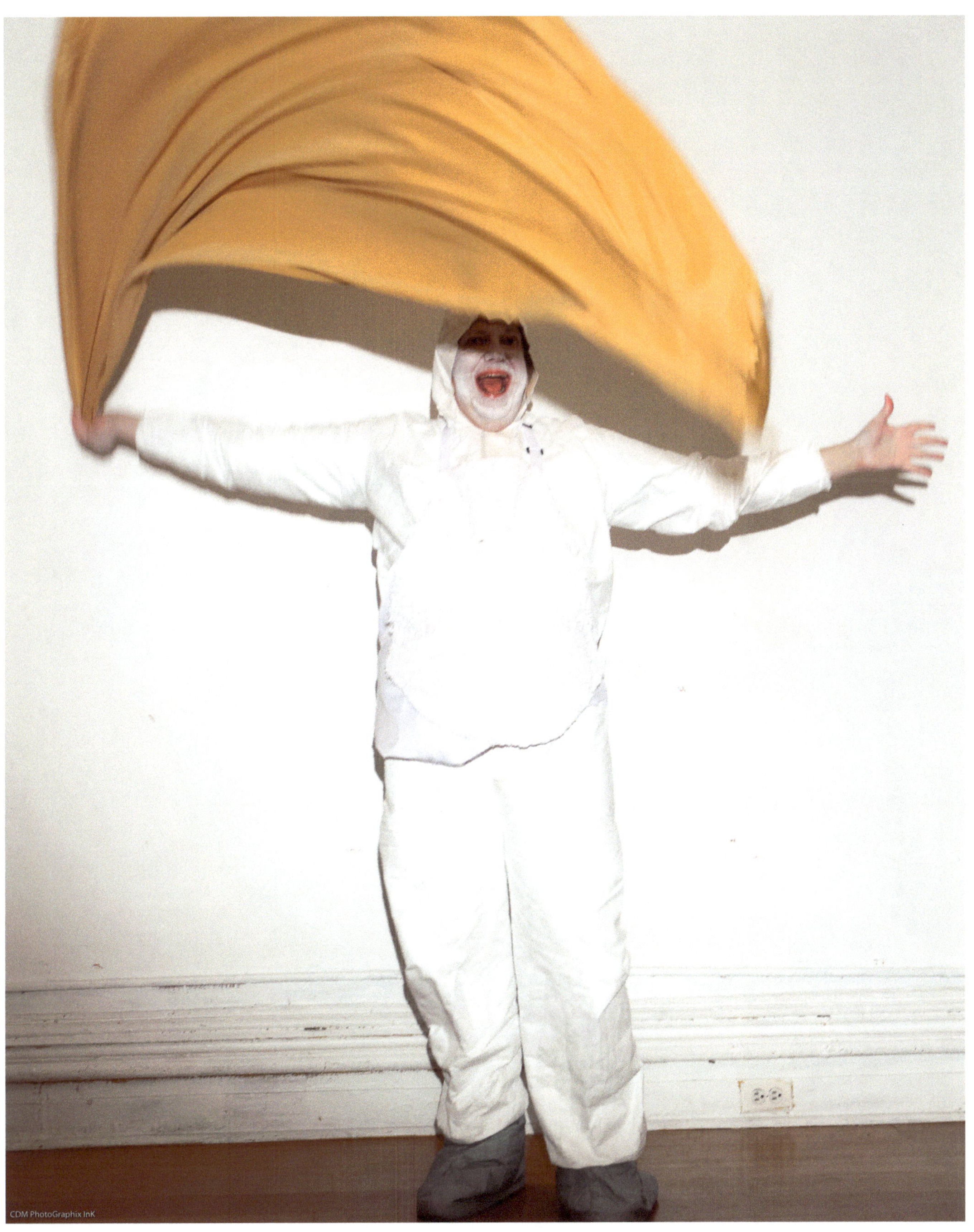

Tony Torn in *Spider Rabbit* by poet Michael McClure, directed by Dan Safer.
Photo by Charles McCain

Senga Nengudi

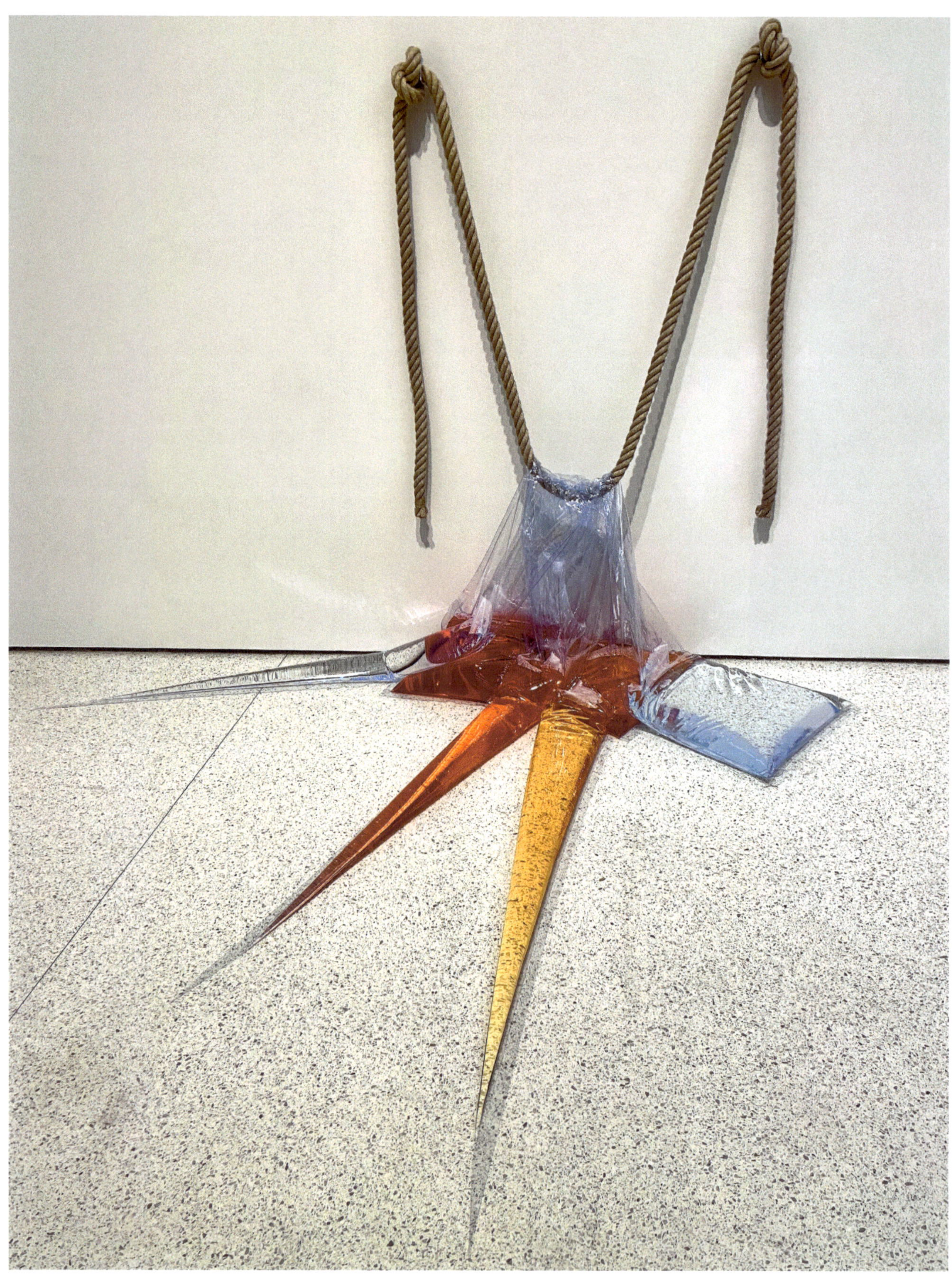

Water Composition I, 1970/2019, vinyl, rope, water, food coloring, A.P. 1/1, ed. of 2.
16   In "Sensory Poetics: Collecting Abstraction." Courtesy of the Solomon R. Guggenheim Museum, NYC.

The day Toni Morrison dies
a resident throws hot joe at a nurse

the Bad Bitch throws a chair through a window,
the pest with cluster B

personality disorders throws herself
from wheelchair to floor.

Elders inspect her bald patch, prophecy
tomorrow's lunch, lasagna you'd mistake

for layers of earth I eat because it's what
a mad Pecola might do in solidarity

I go mad, lose myself for years in Bed
stuy gardens, lead-infused carrots

accused of mercury poisoning
by the CDC who care enough

to write. A pen pal would be nice
says J reading Sula in the restroom

after mid night in solidarity with decay
I declare myself lesbian, radioactive

even before I've stewed the knotweed
of Central Park, my pots lesbian pots

sky a lesbian sky here at the half-life of a woman
budding inside a woman the thirst of a single car

nation with scoliosis swaying like Jack
in a box against the backdrop of the over

heard tracks in solidarity with the dead
my lids drop like gates of a bodega.

I. Can't. Make. The rent. In these ribs, this
wheel of hives, a homo-Ana

—phylaxis

They Live (Laugh, Love)

The way a razor longs for that long wrist.
Or the way a white man loves a white van.
The way that should becomes because they can.
Or the way a black eye looks for its fist.
Or so they say. They talk & talk & twist
every objection like a madman,
sweep your broken bones into a dustpan
of herstory (*history*, they insist).
They're everywhere & nowhere all at once,
skimming the surface yet deep in the blood.
They take for granted all that's the given.
They exist the way a hat wears its dunce.
We are the tides, but they are the flood—
a toxic bloom. An ammunition.

The Book that Burns as Each Page Turns

In the latest twist, the hero is the villain,
while the villain remains the villain; only
their motherland can tell them apart, each
with a face that only a motherland could love
(the fatherland only cares which is his, which
the bastard). Well, there's no accounting for taste,
unlike greed, which accounts for nearly everything.
There is no binary they will not insist on, no
contradiction they will not embrace, no
prodigal son (or daughter) they will not turn away.
They are the firemen willing to stand by
while the flames lick the doorways you loitered in,
& the smoke chokes the family you chose,
saying, *Guess you should have paid your premiums.*
They are the sharp teeth in the nation's jaw,
grinding the ashes in the nation's mouth.

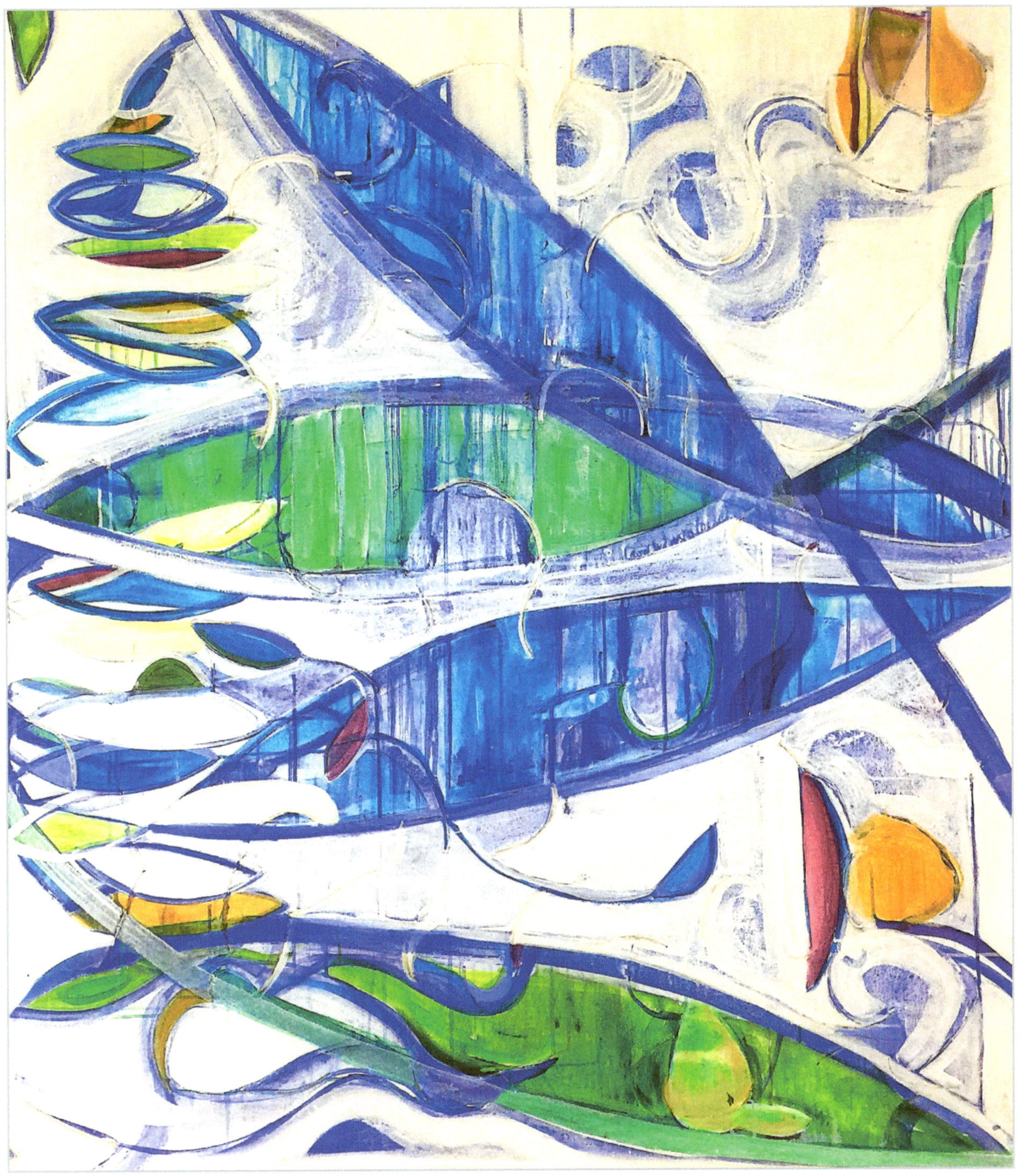

From the Earth to the Sky, pigment, elemental materials, acrylic on canvas, 52 x 60 in.

Wang Ping

Immigrant Can't Write Poetry: Mad Yak Corso

In the courtyard of St. Mark's church
Poets milled around, waiting for the event
Of the year, organized by Poetry Project.
Allen was going to read "Howl."
I was scheduled to read before Allen.
I had spent three weeks writing a poem for this event:
The Song of Calling Souls, story of Chinese
Immigrants who drowned in Rockaway NY
After jumping the ship to run from the cops.
It was a big crowd, with people I knew well—
Lewis, Ron, Ed, Rudy and Yvonne, and people I never met.
Flowers were booming, and the church
Looked beautiful and dignified as usual.

Someone grabbed my legs, shouting
Things I couldn't understand.
I screamed and jumped, but the man
With wild hair held onto my ankles
His body mopping the church yard
As I tried to move away from him.
People were laughing as if it was something normal
Even entertaining, until Allen rushed over
Picked him up and dragged him away.
I heard him say, "Take it easy, Greg.
Go home and sleep it off."
Then he turned to me:
"No worries, Penny. He's harmless.
He's just being Greg Corso."

I didn't know who Greg Corso was.
I thought I didn't know, but my spirit already knew.
I should be startled, but I was not.
No, I was more than startled. I was electrified
Like the first thunderbolt striking winter fields
Where seeds, roots and worms had been awaiting.

That night I read my poem along with Ginsberg.
His "Howl" and my "Song of Calling Souls"
Set the crowd and church on fire.

In St. Paul, I taught "Mad Yak" and "Marriage"
To elite students at an elite college, together with
Ginsberg, Snyder, Kerouac, Waldman, Alexie, Erdrich, Troupe…
Till I heard Greg passed in Robbinsdale, 20 miles from me
Till I got booted out for teaching things "unsafe"
And "inappropriate," for "appropriating Native and Black
Cultures" as a Chinese, and "anti-white," and worse,
"Manipulating students' emotions with poetry."

But nothing can put out the fire and thunder
Gregory Corso ignited in me
As he grabbed my legs and mumbled magic
Into my soul at St. Mark's Church.
He was blessing me with his essence.
He was passing his torch to a girl from China
Who is just as untamable as Mad Yak Corso
Writing and teaching poetry in English
Defying the mocking from elite critics:
"Immigrants can't write poetry."

Kevin Opstedal

ONCE UPON A TIME IN SHAOLIN

Spinning the Wheel of Outrageous Fortune
beneath a bubble-wrapped sky
worth its weight in silver spoons

Sunbleached Chrome & I Told You So
A cool breeze kicks sand across the sidewalk
      like a ghost mule dragging The Cantos
            70 foggy miles up the coast

The Sound of Waves Breaking to Exonerate
the Sacred Pyramids & Taco Stands
highlighted on the
chemical map
along w/me & you & Blind Willie McTell

A Rendering Unencumbered by Sobriety
carefully set at a certain angle slant
among bird shadows in the cypress

Winner Winner Chicken Dinner
It's 10 minutes to sunset
     the burnt pink & turquoise sky is
           turning somersaults
& you're easily dazzled

Christy Rupp

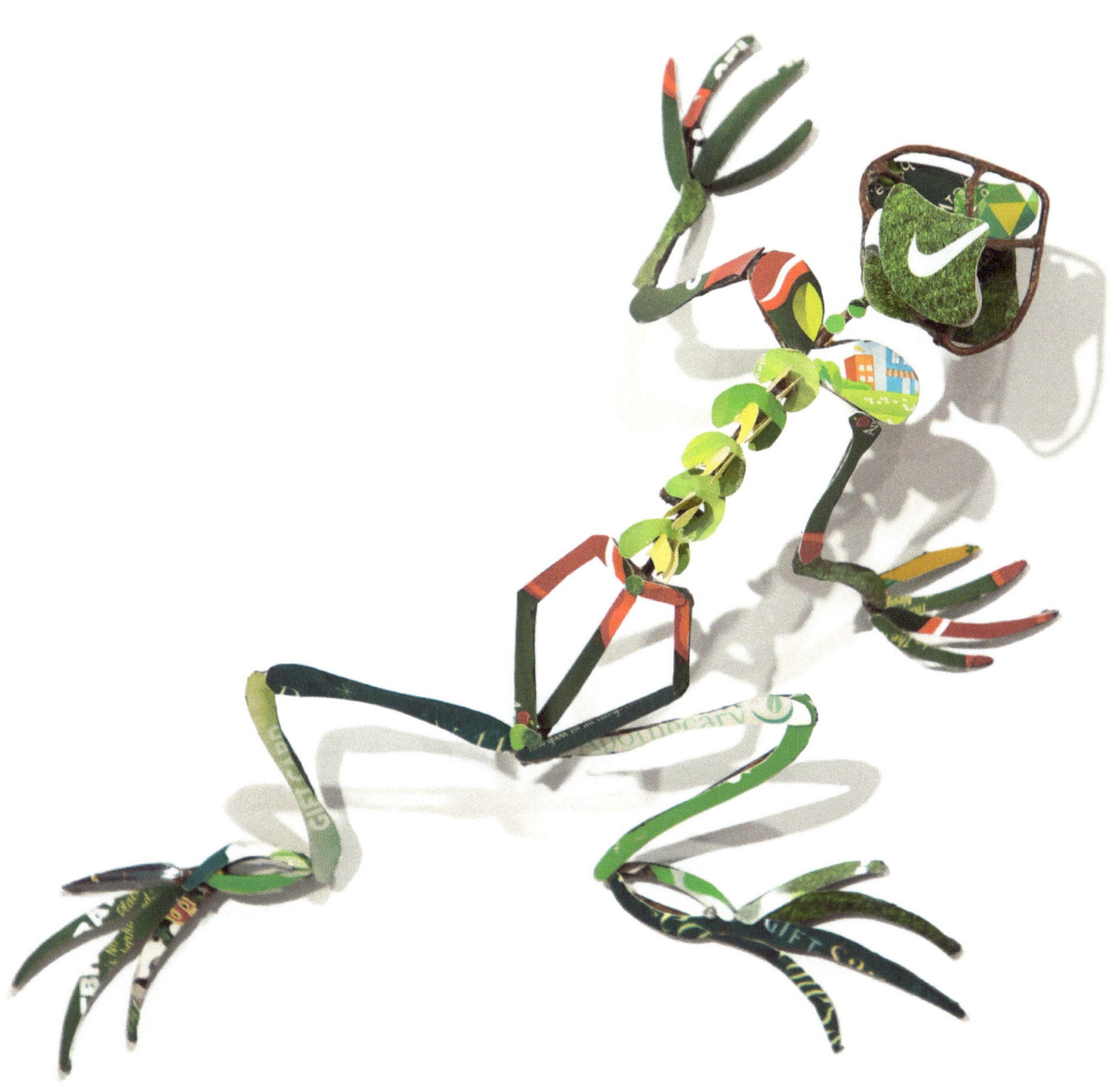

From "CHRISTY RUPP, OTHERED." Courtesy of Howl! Arts

Rose Hartman

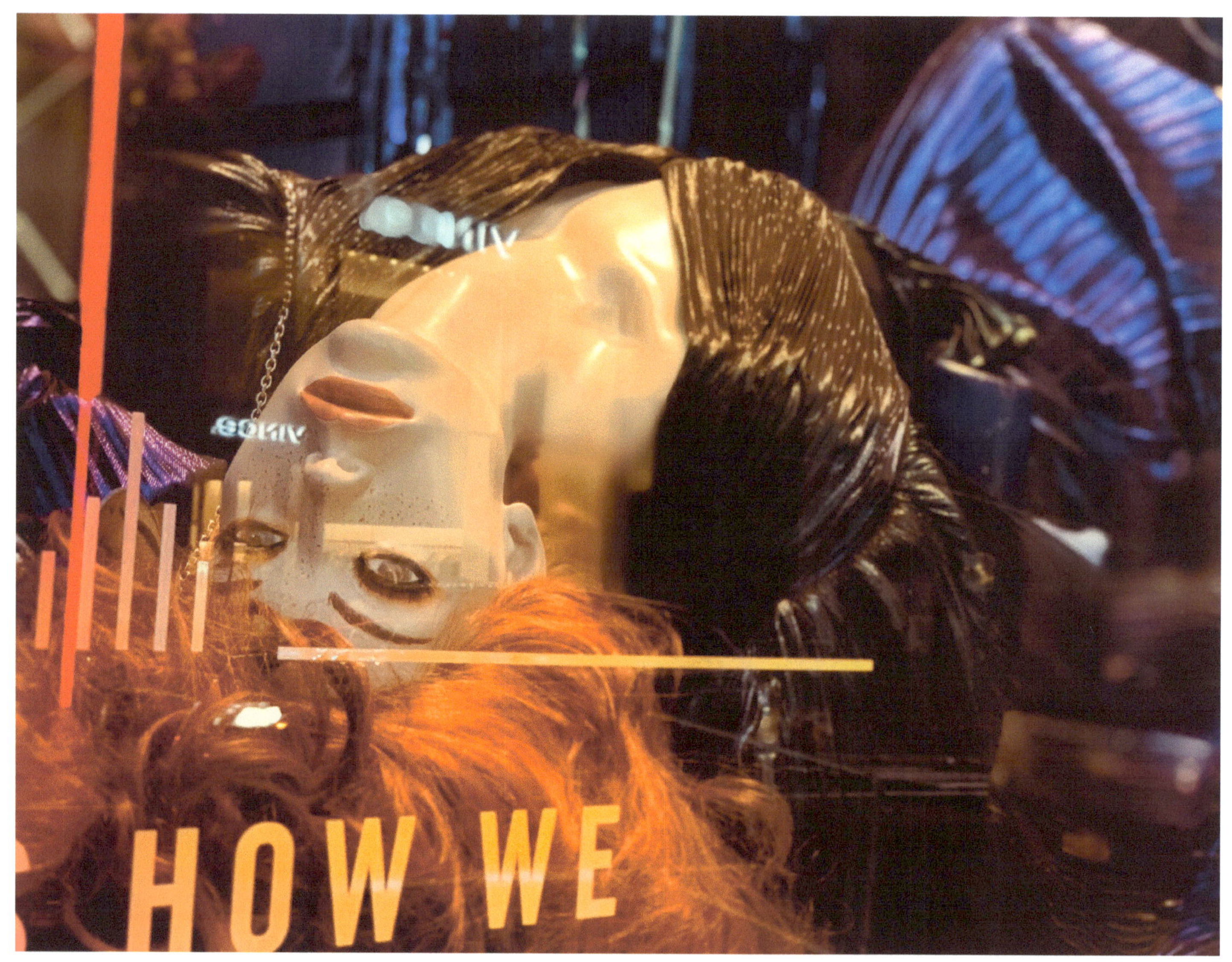

Photograph from *Dreams on Sale*

Allan Kaplan

Popeye's Off Spinach

One barbell and all a them
bottles ya see 'specially
the *Mega* make cudgels
a me arms.

As I asked me pal,
"Wimpy, how are them
flappy arms a yours
gonna knock
any heavies out a are way

Ya needs those nutrients.
A big salad won't give
ya *madness and faith.*"

Any Which Way

N

"If my talented wife my schoolyard hoops
my 401K my hay fever is only a dream
why don't you wake me up?" "I'm trying."

W

"Take off your clothes. Who's that
 in the mirror?" "A lonely stranger."
"Give him a hug. Take him home.

E

"She's with me. Oh, she's hot!" "Wow!"
"She's gone. She was so hot." "I'm sorry."
"She's back. I'm burned out!" "I love a farce."

S

"Bad would just stop stealing if Bad
 would only look to our sweet Good."
"Too late. Bad's hooked on Blood."

Ilka Scobie

Aquarius

For Janine Pommy Vega 1942-2010

Whoever headlined your *New York Times* obit
—which you would have liked, death notice in
the paper of record—
Never really knew you
Certainly never loved you
You were called "a restless poet"
As if you had not homesteaded a Willow cabin,
Up the steepest ungravelled incline,
Ice-slicked for long dark frozen months
Your nearest neighbor a hibernating brown bear

Restless? Because you fearlessly scaled mountains
From Nepalese summits to Catskill's gentle heights
Because you trekked the Amazon
Brought poetry to migrant camps
Or strode into jails to spread the Word

Over a decade that you have been gone
O Janine, perhaps a gift that you've missed
America's facist flirtation
And with your expansive heart and uncensored mouth,
you never could stay silent.
They called you a witch because you sang incantations
A sexual explorer, they called you a whore

I called you mentor, sister, friend
When asked if you had any children,
You recited the names of your poetry books

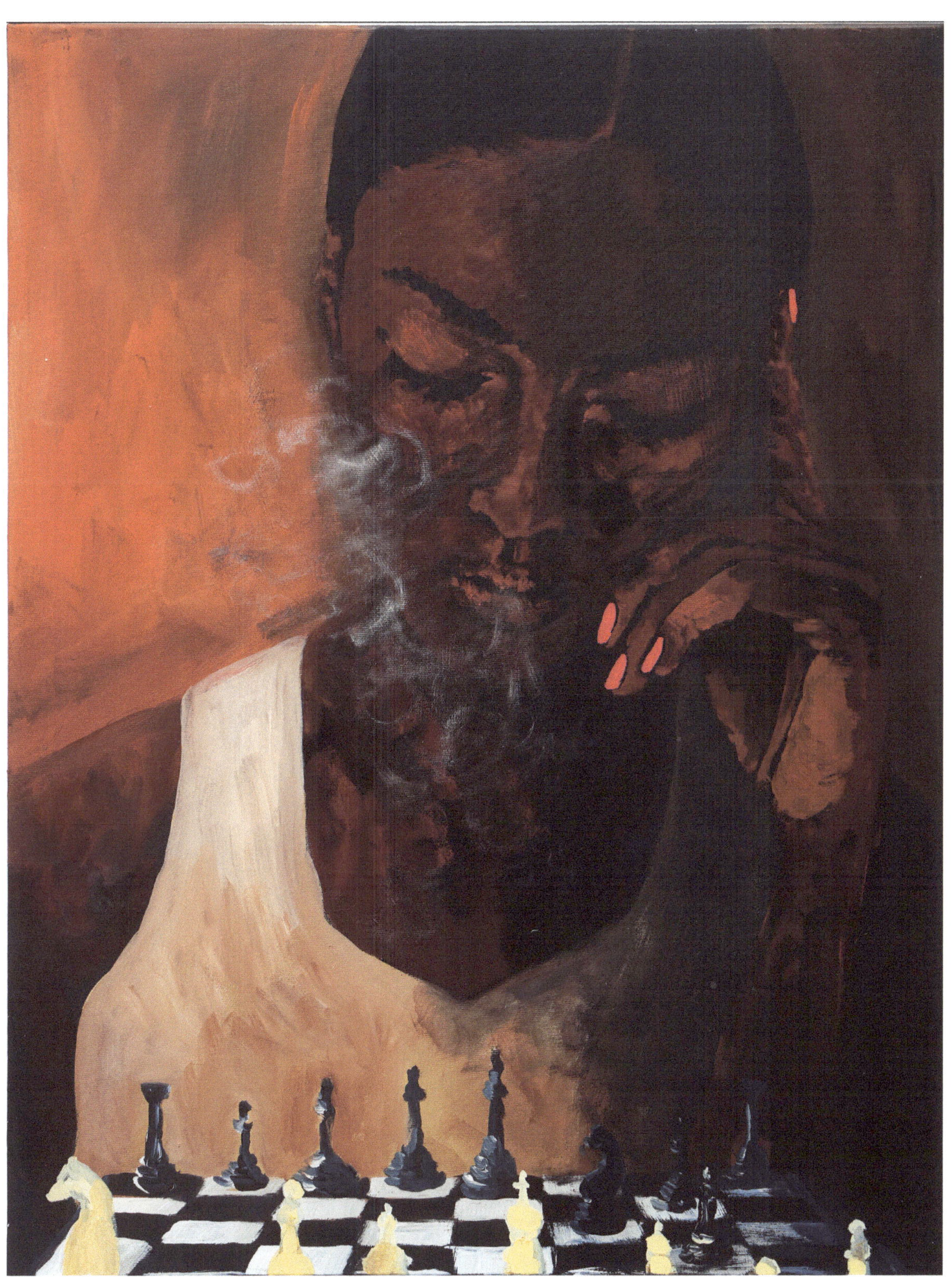

No Cross No Crown, 2022, acrylic on canvas, 24 x 18 in.
Photo Credit: Luis Corzo. Courtesy of Nicola Vassell Gallery.

Albert Dépas

The Dark Side of Me

The dark side of me
is buried into the light
that others do not see;
a mirrored image
of black matter from the universe;
rays piercing through
the ignorant, arrogant egotist
of those claiming to be righteous.

The dark side of me,
dark as the midday sun
of the summer solstice
stands high while others run
with a shameful, bigoted notice.

The dark side of me
sits calmly as a prism
separating the wisdom
of ancient days
from the cracking noise
of eroded wisdom teeth.

Though the dark side of me
is as dark as a mystery
yet to be conceived,
the bright light of others,
in its pseudo-perception,
finds its sustenance
from the core of my darkness.

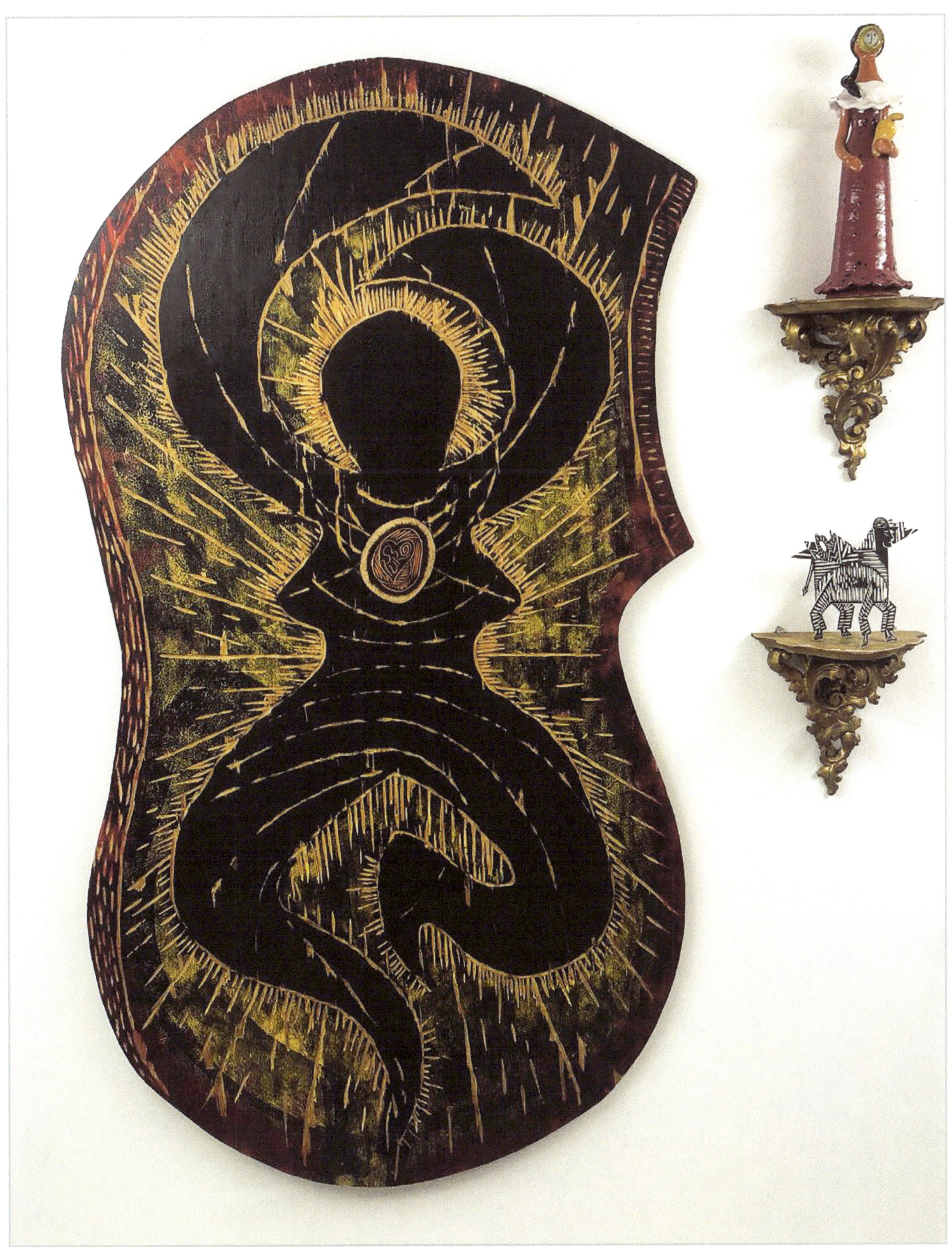

Corazon Puro, 2019,
Acrylic, carved wood, woodcut print, ceramic figure, shelves, 60 x 48 in.

Thaddeus Rutkowski

Tunnel Vision

The light at the end of this tunnel is blinding.
The tunnel was used by trains
going from one side of a mountain to the other.
The tube is huge, almost a perfect cylinder;
the opening at each end is almost a perfect circle,
held up by fitted boulders radiating from a keystone.

You'll need no light other than daylight to guide you.
And if you sit to rest and forget yourself,
you might be buzzed by flies, bitten by mosquitoes,
or visited by the bats that roost in the roof,
but you will not be run over by a train.
The rail tracks are long gone.

WHO'S CRYING NOW?

When you read your poetry in public,
do you want to make the audience cry,
or do you want to make yourself cry?

If the audience cries,
it may be a sign that what you're saying
is very good—or very bad.

If you cry, you'll reveal yourself
to be a sensitive person, one who cares deeply
about any and all painful things.

You should make a gesture, while you cry,
of drawing a bow across the strings
of the world's smallest violin.

Maybe the idea is to make everyone cry:
you and everyone in the audience, all weeping together.
A good cry never hurt anyone.

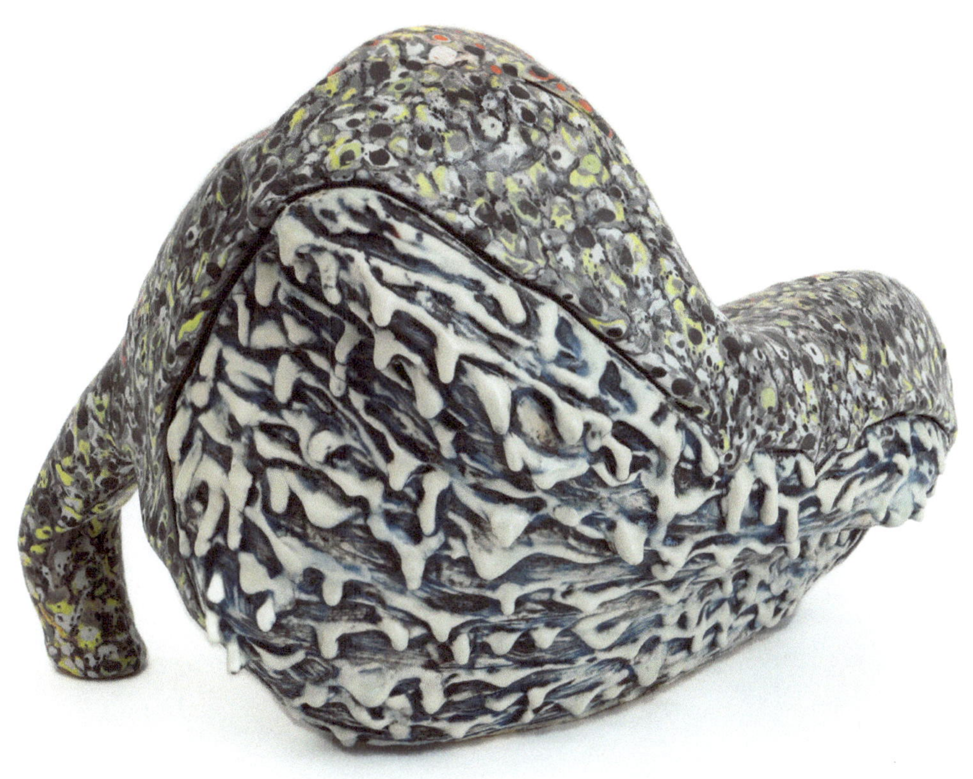

Both Sides Now 2, 2021, glazed ceramic, 8 x 9.5 x 7 in.
Courtesy the artist and Patricia Sweetow Gallery, Los Angeles

Bonny Finberg

Avian Love Song

His echo,
stone gray and flanked
by trees fastened to the ground,
cemented in their small brown squares,
wild roots below,
hidden,
an undiscovered text.
He waits.

Her answer, plaintive,
soft and foreign,
not the one he hoped,
the jeweled clarion,
others,
but not the one,
the lyric withered,
music weakened,
went.

Here, *here*, he sings.
Here, *here*. Here, *here*. Here, *here*."

Then her distant,
Come, come. Come, come.

Yes, yes, yes.

Her increase,
nearer,
their ancient chorus:
Here, *here*.
Here, *here*.
Here, *here*.
Yes, yes, yes.
Two rivers rushing,
confluent,
Here, *here*.
Here, *here*.
Here, *here*.
Yes, yes, yes.
Come away.

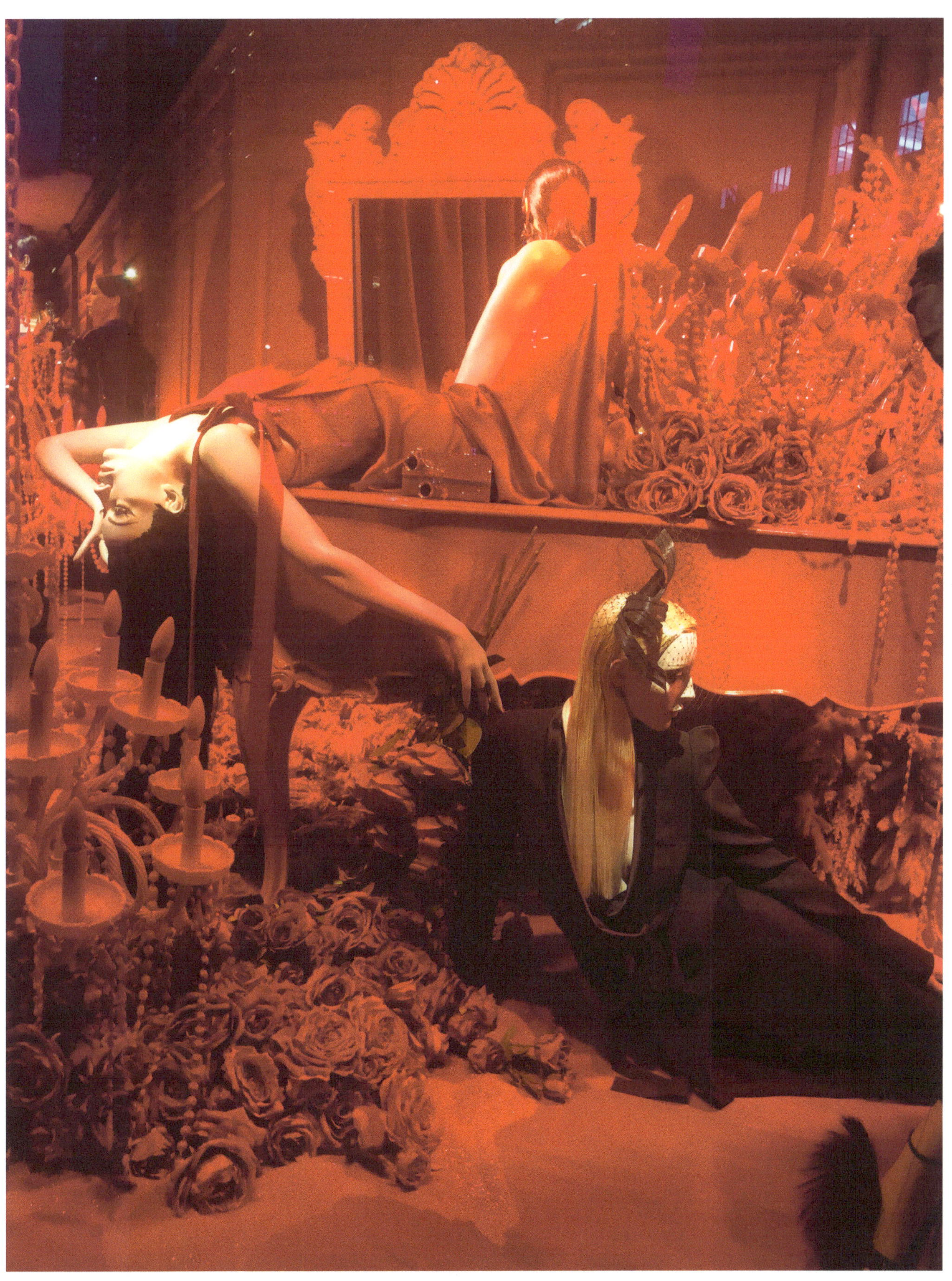

Photograph from *Dreams on Sale*

Judith Simonian

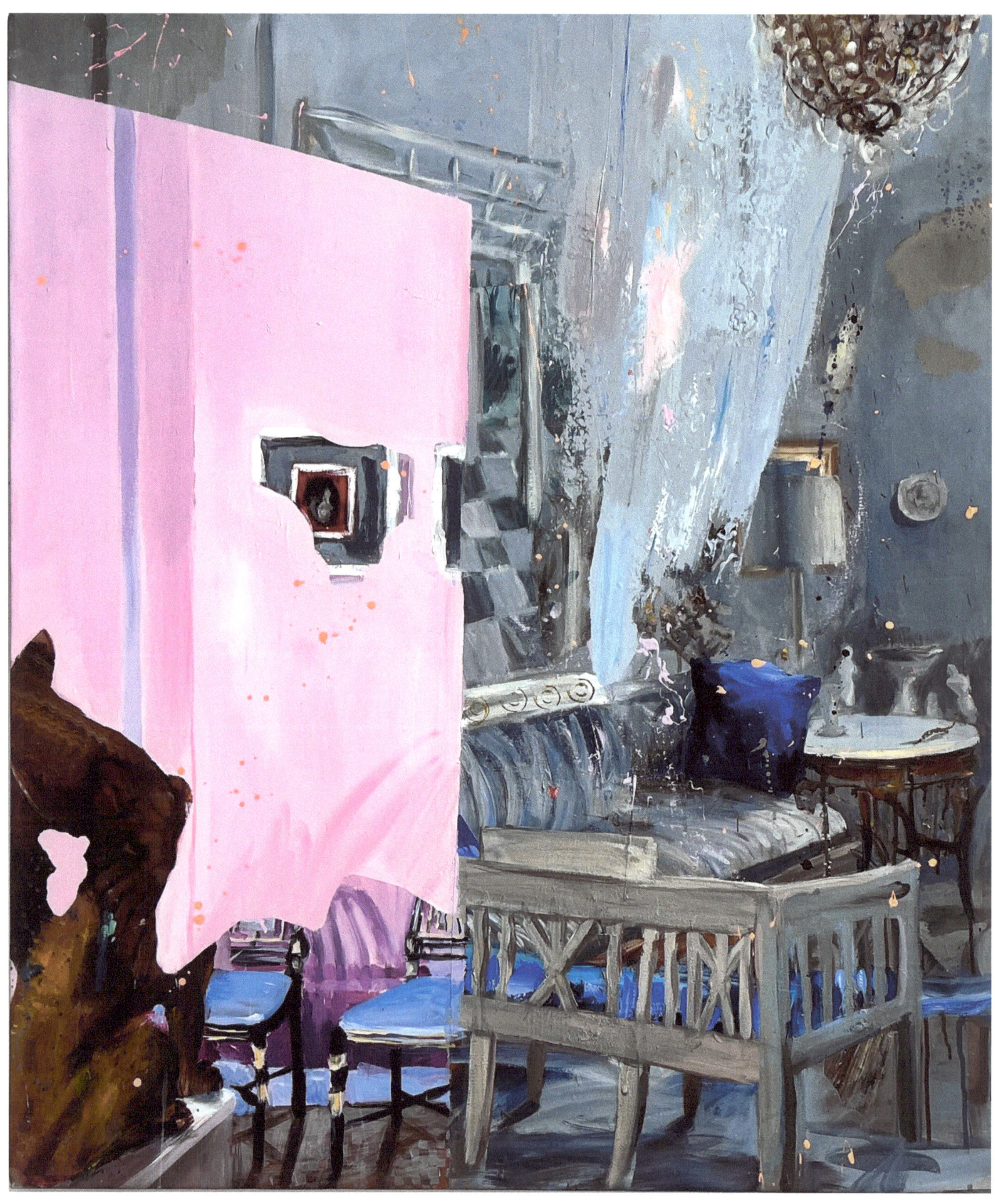

Pink and Gray Empire, 2013, acrylic on canvas 50 x 42 in.
in 'PLUSH: Paintings by Judith Simonian 2010-2022 at 1 Gap Gallery

Lovers in Black

After Marc Chagall

Compare us to the couple kissing
in Chagall's India-ink drawing.

She bears down on him ghoulish and proud, dark-eyed.
He hesitates.

Chagall's postcard adorns my cabinet.
You and me—our dark theatrical days.

Chassidic souls brimming with song. Russian nights,
Belted drinks. On the roof you parted

my legs beyond the frum family's barbeque
Jostling love and fecklessness.

Chagall's young man turns into a beast.
Their lips brush. He clutches fire.

She fits like a card in his pocket.
Love and art—such fruitful madness—how do they endure?

Flying cows and chortling roosters, kisses that miss the mark.
Victory obtained in black. Plush. Obscure.

Bonny Finberg

Apology

I'm sorry. Please accept my humblest apologies.
I'm here to say you can't escape the fact
conception births belief,
creates the word,
creates the world,
can only hope it shields your ass,
perceives beyond your eyes.

But hope, like all it dictates dies,
the sooner gone, the closer to our nature,
permission then to walk away, to die alone,
to leave our doppelgangers in our dust,
to turn away and rise above this vaguely proffered earth,
which something perfect bore,
where childish lies of immortality then grew.

Questionnaire

Which is better—cake or cookies?
Would you rather swim in the sea or an indoor pool?
How do you like your cheese—soft or firm?
Do you take your coffee black, with milk or cream?
How do you rate your lovers—brains or beauty?
Where would you rathr be—in bed or the beach?
What is the better way—love or duty?
Who would you rather kiss—liar or snake?
How to murder a tyrant—blow torch or poison?
Who do you ask for help—God or the bank?
Where do you go for love—Heaven or Hell?
How would you rather die—in rage or despair?
What is your favorite drug—love or pain?
How did you lose your faith—in love or defeat?
How might you gain it back—in victory or love?
Who do you know the best—enemy or friend?
How would you cast your legacy—in thought or love?
When do you know the point—at birth or death?
How can you find your way—by heart or mind?

Elizabeth Schwaiger

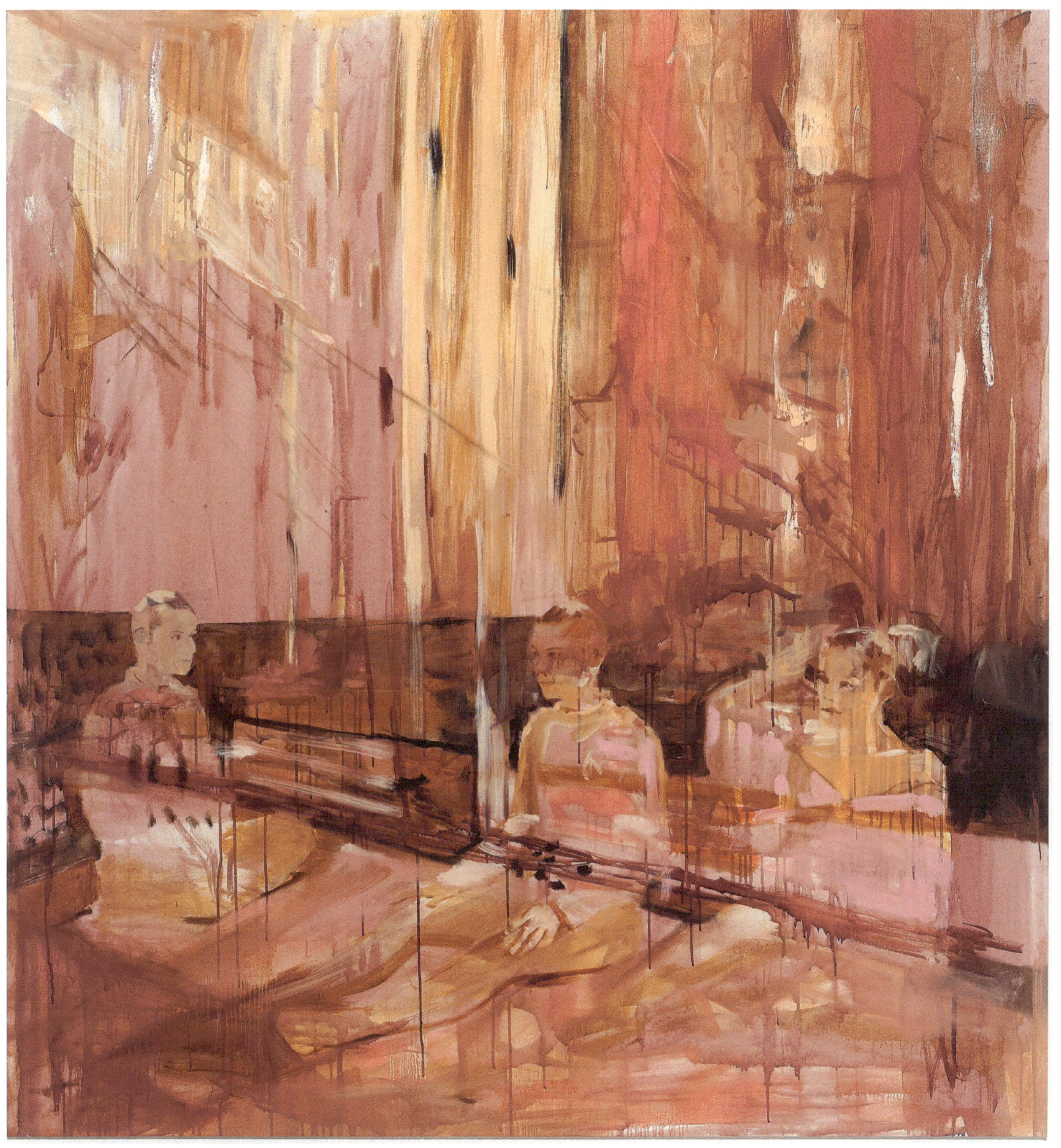

Restless Warmth, 2020, acrylic, watercolor, and oil on canvas, 66 x 61 in.
Courtesy of the artist and Jane Lombard Gallery.

Danielle McKinney

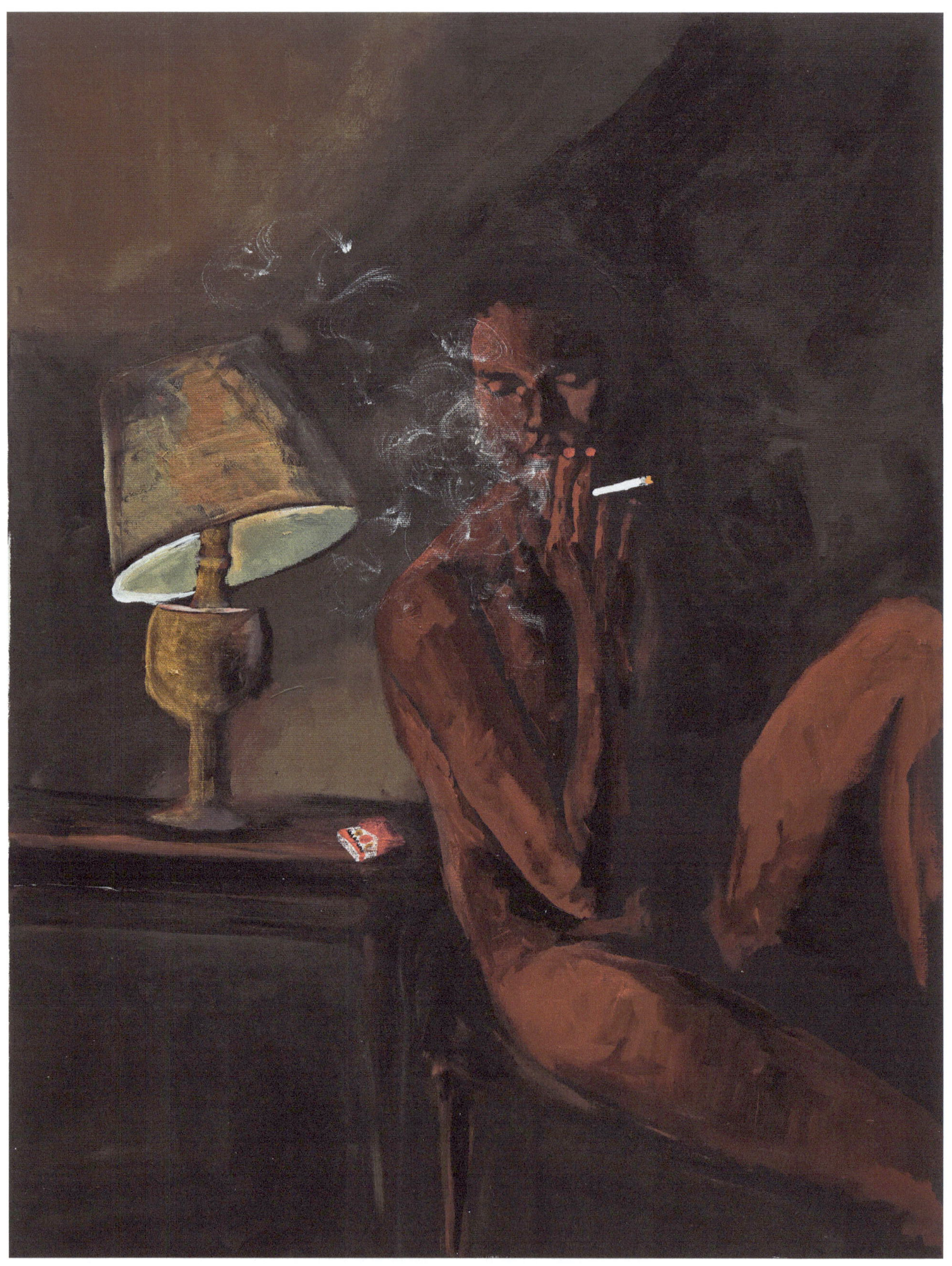

Moth, 2022, acrylic on canvas, 24 x 18 in.
Photo Credit: Luis Corzo. Courtesy of Nicola Vassell Gallery.

Concrete Gehenna

I.

She lives a life defined
        by—the words
begin with a hiss—
        suffering and spine.
She delivers His message
        to ears open
and closed. Manhattan.
        The Bronx. Brooklyn.
Queens. Her pulpit: any
        corner at any
intersection. Today,
        Friday, 6 p.m.,
rush hour in midtown,
        under late autumn's
early nightfall, she
        declaims, with a
prophet's fire, chapter
        and verse at
the Church of Broadway
        and W. 48th Street.
Who told thee that
        thou wast naked?
For the financial advisors
        and tourists from
Iowa her Old Testament
        exhortations are
a strained organ in a
        performance of
an atonal work called
        Noise Metropolis.

II.

Her home is a walk-up
        that nobody sees,
fourth floor, down the hall,
        three rooms at
the back of the building.
        Where she has no
TV or radio, no laptop or
        phone. Where on
the walls unframed pictures
        of a fig tree hang.
Where she feeds herself
        apples, grapes,
and pomegranate seeds.
        Where she opens
the cage on the floor,
        pulls out a white
rat, and feeds the snake
        in the terrarium.
Where she sits at
        the kitchen table,
naked, opens her Bible
        to Genesis 2, and
rereads, night after night,
        her life story.

Emily Cheng

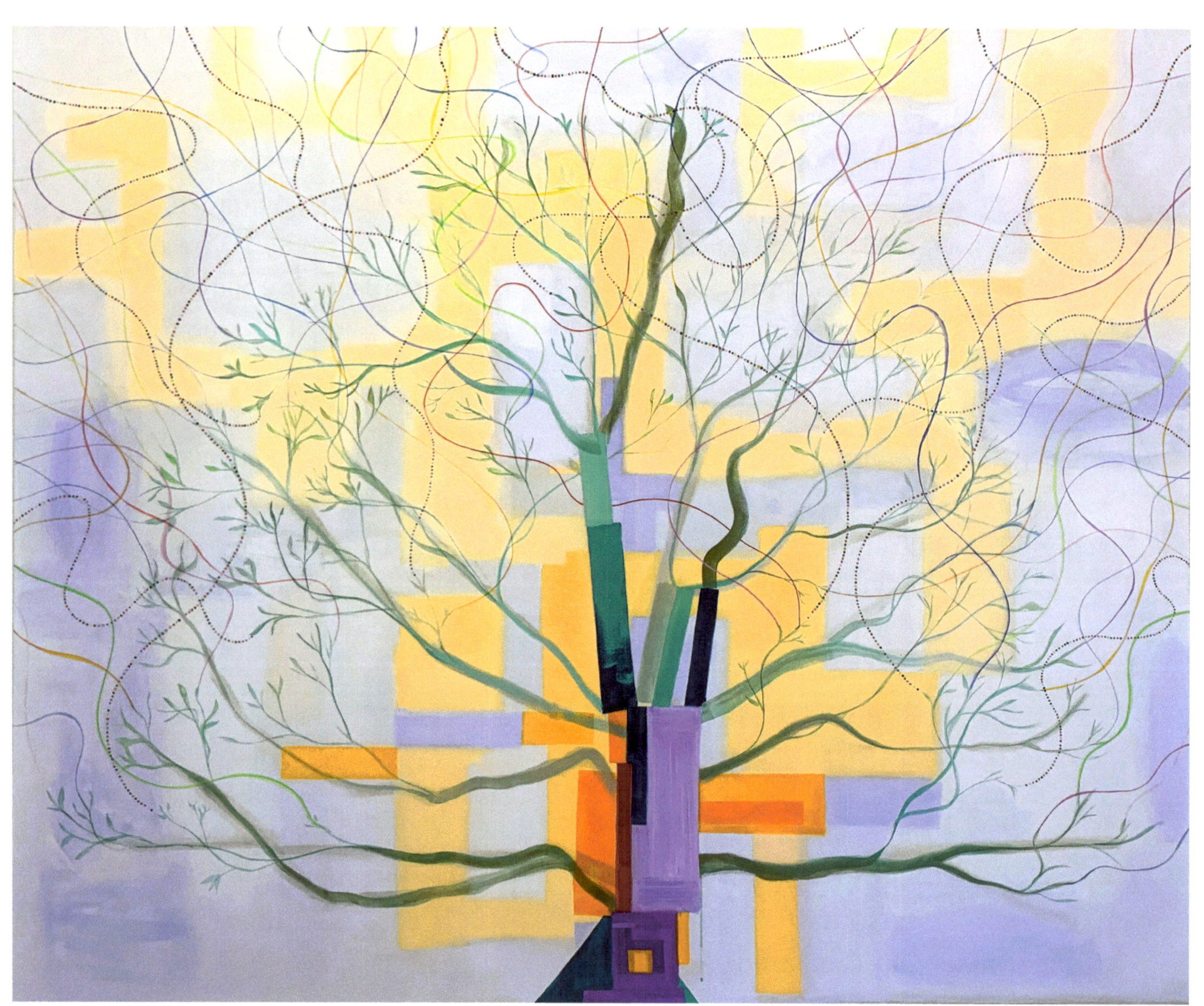

Nine Worlds, 2020, flasche on canvas, 70 x 80 in.

"INFINITE CONSANGUINITY BEARS US"
— *Hart Crane*

Monsoons take us home
To Monzon on Wide World of Sports
For the reckoning and answer

Hope of ether
And old time doggone

Force fields of sanity
And longtime implicated
Eaten holistically
Breadbasket of panjandrum

We leave peopled for residence
Leave them the sausage positives
There Rangooned
Who hula'd
Hellbent on pork bellies
And isolated solvents
In this our unspecific

Yes to all of the above sandwiches
So it is the rice of acknowledgeable Cincinnati

Yes to all of the above sandwiches
So it is in the infomercial of our daisies
So it is without the thick walls of finance
So it is ... pearly and soft
Frank in the form of pellicles
So it is teething holiday sandwiches
Draking on the hustings
And otherwise polishing the rightful barbershop
In this on and off again (sizing arena, right?)
So it is
So it is
Yes to all of the Telemann for your habits
Yes to all of the Rosenkranz with a cigar

Leslie Prosterman

Black Ice Rose

Northern lights verglazed the moon:

Snow cones

that were veins of frost lace over

past nights that never happened

yet

cardinal hugely puffed up for winter hopping around in my garden contentedly
searching for kernels to get her through the winter or through the long flight

anyway,

low to the ground and enjoying what is there.

A giant star died in a supernova.

This is my rime, my film, my repeated snapshot,

my repeated image of you.

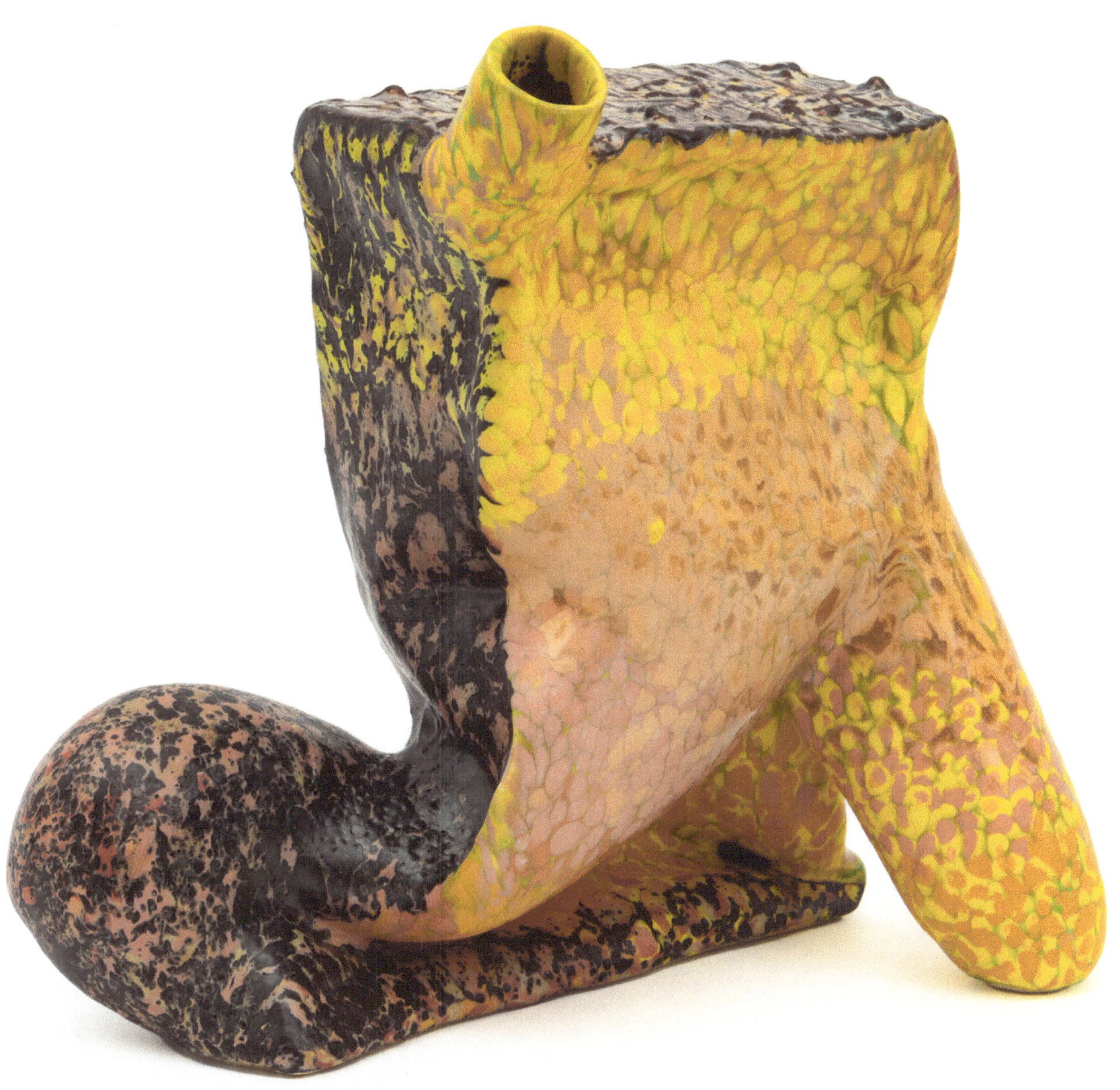

Both Sides Now 4, 2022, glazed ceramic, 8 x 8 x 6 in.

Moses Ros

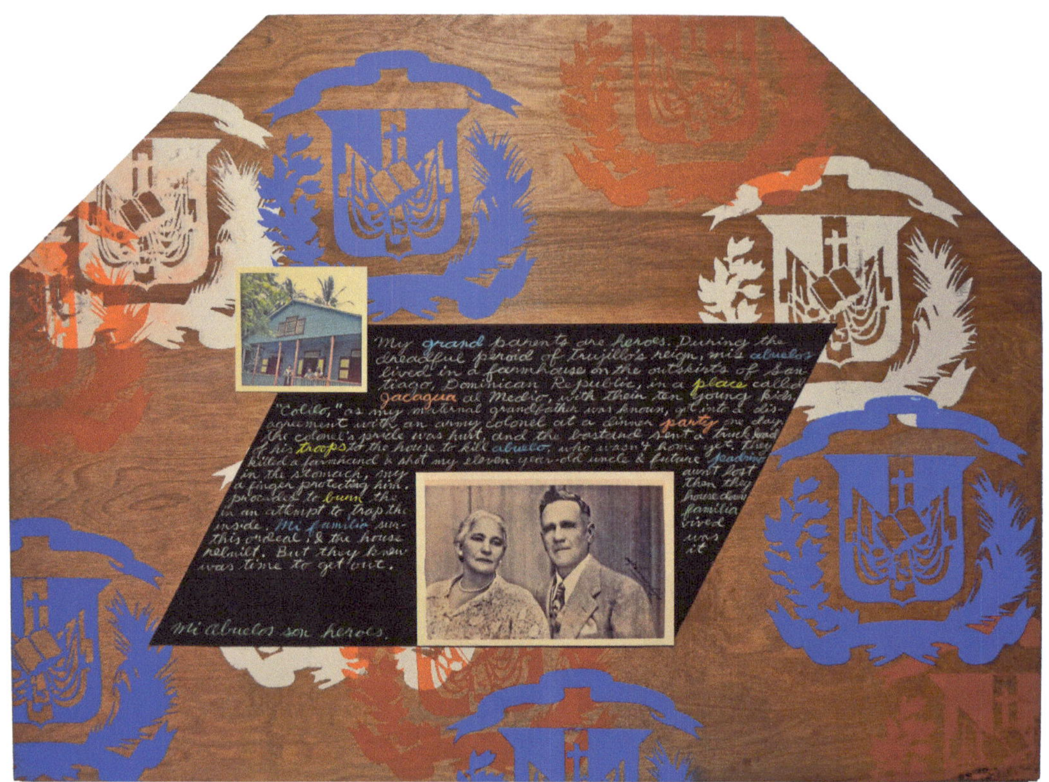

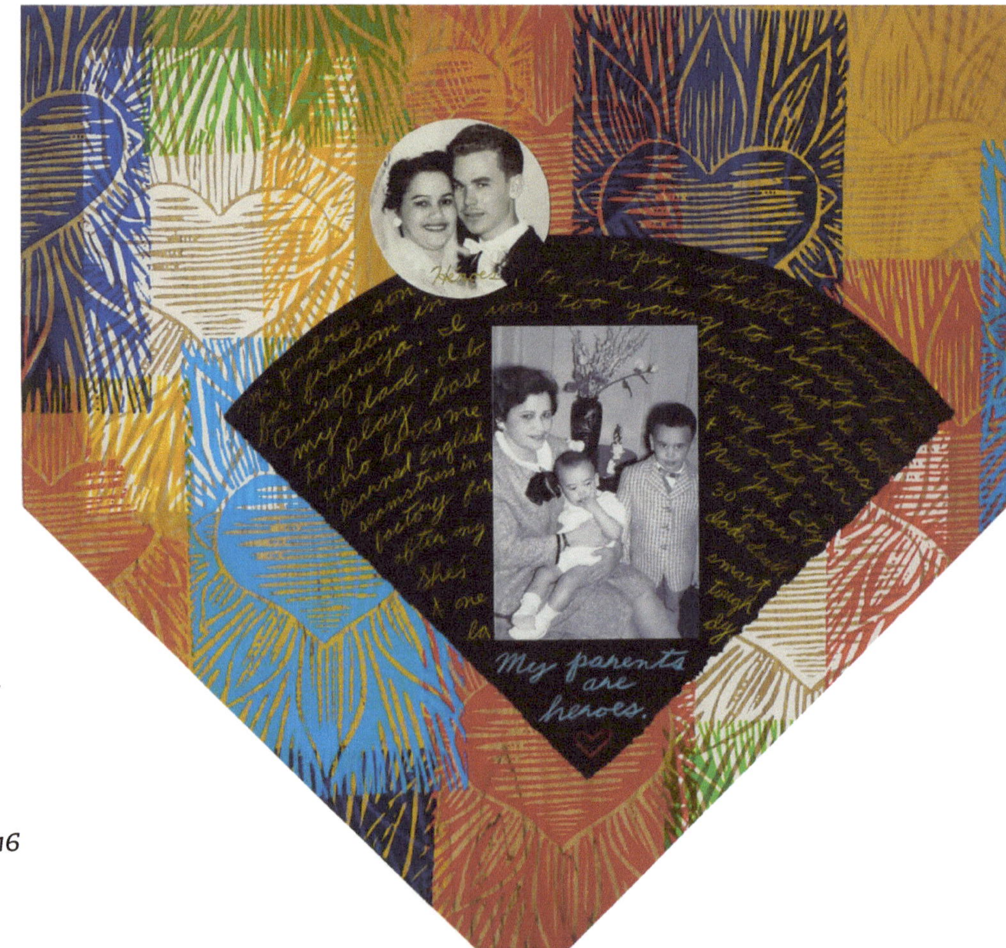

Top:
Honoring My Grandparents, 2016,
Wood, screen printing, photo-
graphs, paper collage, 24 x 30 in.

Right:
Honoring My Mother & Father, 2016
Wood, screen printing, photo-
graphs, paper collage, 22 x 22 in.

At the Tomb of the Unknown Feeling

Imagine reading the suicide notes
written by those who will live forever,
the dull irony of small talk, weather,
the dead child on which Eternity dotes.
No one says, *a rising tide floods all boats*,
except for the hole, that bottomless never.
The waitress asks, *Naugahyde or pleather?*
Is it a tumor, this lump in my throat?

As a child, I hugged my Nauga & spoke
in his voice, a voice of gravel & light.
We were born the same year, but I'm stuck here;
he's trapped on eBay beneath money's cloak.
Memory is a form of second sight:
loss, immortal, & the strangeness of tears.

Kevin Opstedal

CALCULATING THE DRIFT

A drive up the coast
behind the wheel of an awkward silence
doesn't allow for the
heavy ordinance

nor the charming way the woman
      beside you bites her lips when
            you speed-shift around those blind curves
                singing off-key

The doctor says it's
bad for my thermostat
but I say it isn't the song so much as
how you sing it

      Pomp & circumstantial evidence
         racing past the
            Department of Planned Obsolescence

& less than a mile from there it
all turns to glass
            which shatters when you
hit the high notes

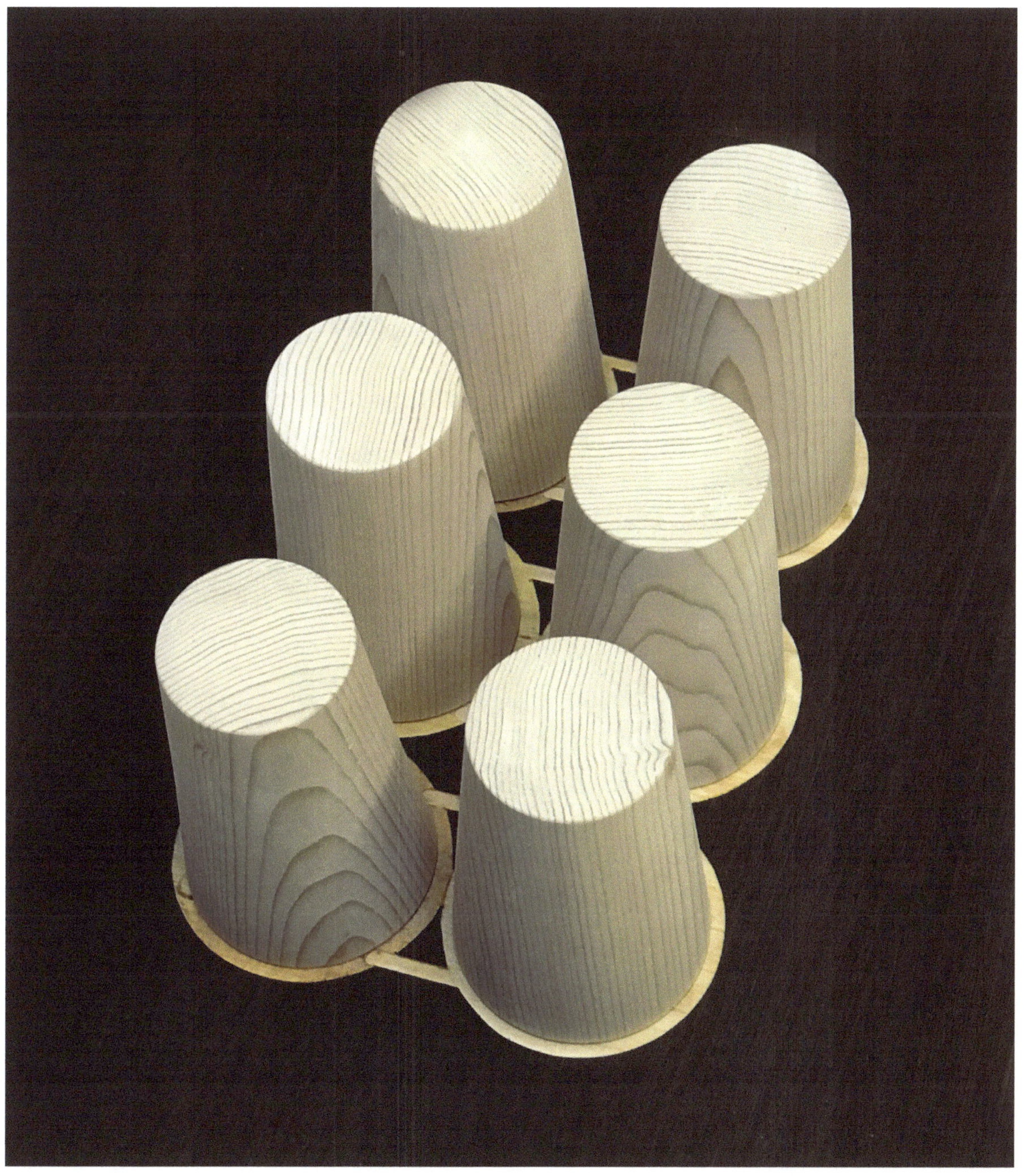

Six Glasses, 2021, pine and wenge plywood, 16 x 20 x 6 1/2 in.

Lydia Cortes

Not for Nothings

But my father
Worked hard
Bit the bullets
There had always
Been more
Than one in PR
On
Delancey in the Jewish
Cafeteria swelter
To grind the grind
Filing down the soul
Washing pots
Chopping beets
Onions y papas
All for his nenes

Us the 3 belles
Of Williamsburg
Later Fort Greene
Down the block
Pratt Instituted
Gated manicured
Better than lacquered
Nails and bullets and
    bullcrap
Being held back

The us
Allowed to live in
The beginnings of
Dilapidation

Still we could stare
Through through Pratts
    iron bars
Barely enough to
See feel how others
Studied we studied the
Them from the outside

We played in
The open cycloned
Playground for all
When the Police Athletic
    League
Counselors came
Around in listless
Long days of
Apartment suffocation

The PAL gal Noreen
Was kind and fat
Taught us to braid
Raffia strands make
Keychains for Papi
Y Mami chains for
Ourselves
for the keys
Around our necks
To get in
To get into our
Apartment when
She wasn't home
When she went
To the bodega
With the 3 stacked
Fiambreras of enameled
Metal to keep the heat in
To bring Papi
His Saturday
Rich communion
Arroz con habichuelas
Quizas con un pedacito
De carne si habia
Una vez y dos son trés

Pero nosotros éramos
En total 5 en Familia
Con un niño un poquito
Abnormal but beautiful
Y Mami y Papi

Una vez y dos éramos
Tres niños one a
Gorgeosity of a little
Long awaited
Boy without words
But full of rocking
And finger snapping
    swaying

Musiquita la notas
Invisibles por dentro

Cómo like hidden
Sharp teeth after
They sliced through
Bleeding gums
Finally allowed
To come in
Come in helped
You are welcomed
Like the tough meat
We sometimes had
Not allowed to
Spit out despite
The gristle
Too tough
For barely
Apparent
Teeth

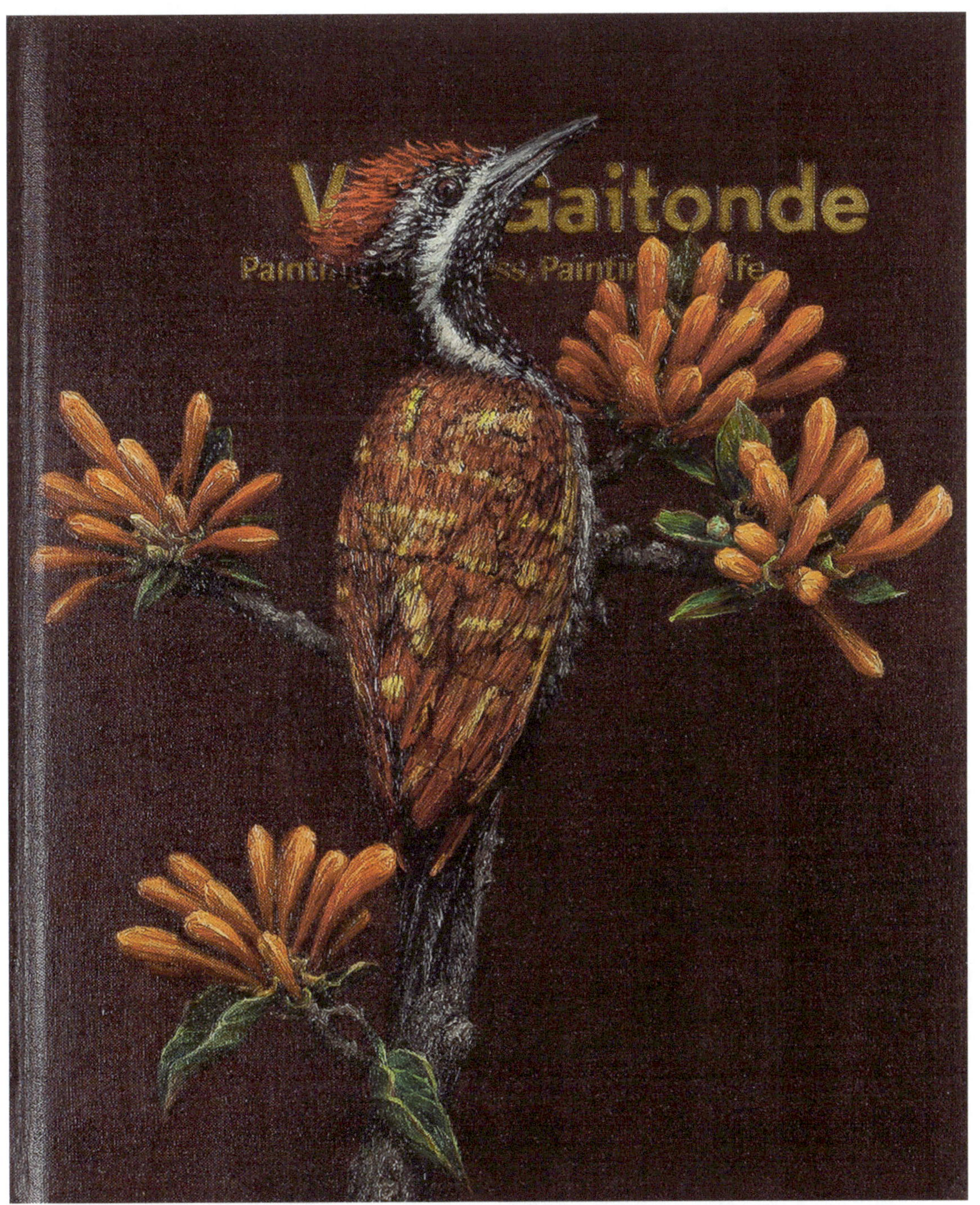

Gaitonde Flameback, detail. Courtesy of Marc Straus Gallery

Cara Galowitz

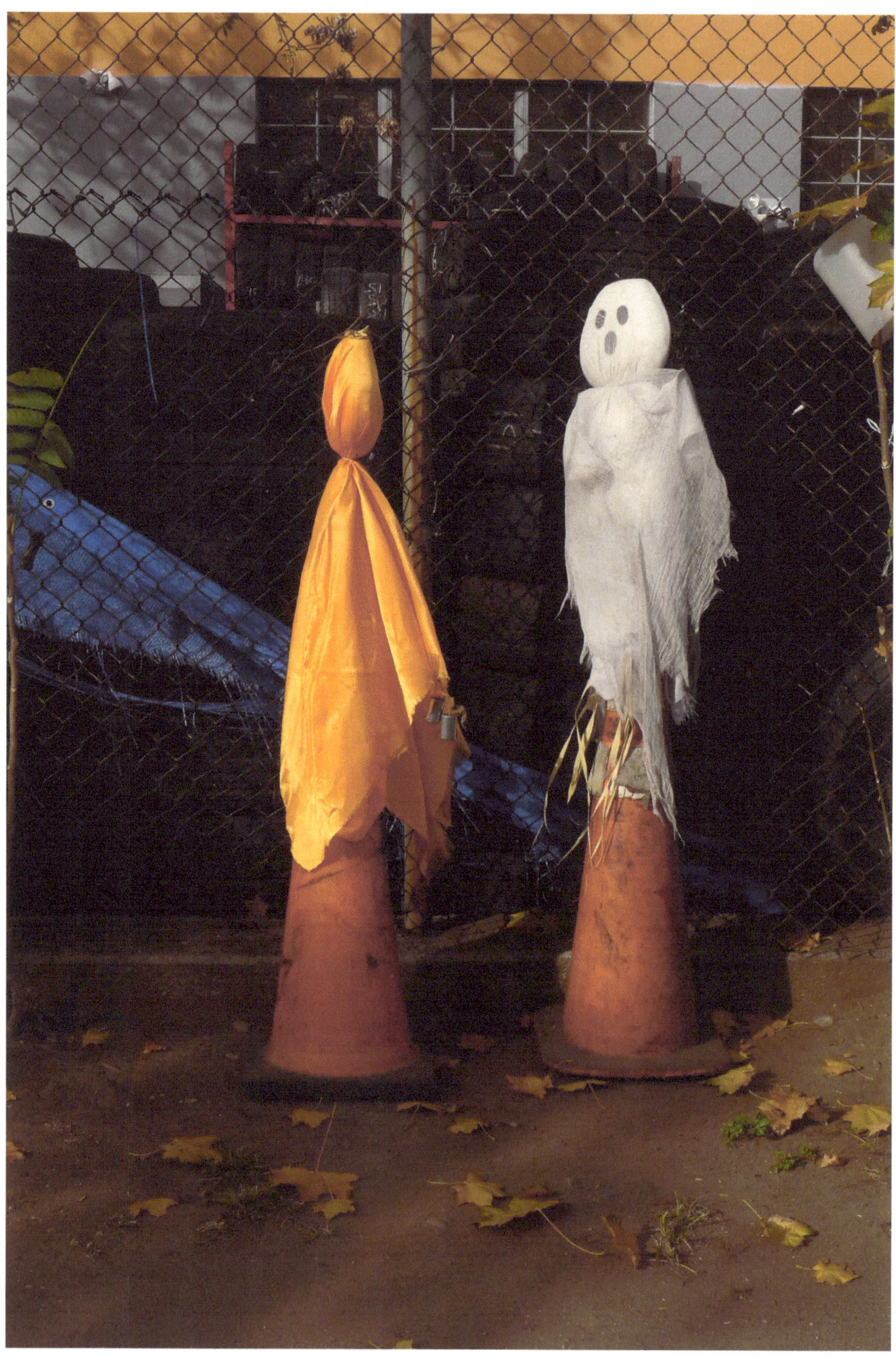

Untitled, 2014, archival digital print, 11 x 14 in.

SENSATIONS

My PYRAMID

I built the Pyramids
Stone by stone
Brick by brick
I scorch the sand
With thoughts Of
The hear after

Tradition

If I sit
In the same chair
You sat in
That's tradition

His X

His X never said
He could use her name
To mark the spot

9

9+9=18
18+18=36
36+36=72
9+72=81
Once I was 81
Not no more

Intransient

He was intransient
Until
He found
Out
What
The word meant

Mobilize

Mobilize
Mobilize
Mobilize
The Greeks
Are coming

No Title

OH, childhood
Find your nipples
And ride the high tide
Of growth

Of secular
Petals
There are
Blossoms

Travel Guide

Never go to
Dublin
London
Paris
Madrid
Or
Rome
by yourself

Male Talk

Header & footer
He's a beauty

Reviews

A SEARING SEER RESEEN

by Ilka Scobie

DIANE DI PRIMA: TWO TRIBUTES

My first Diane di Prima book was *This Kind of Bird Flies Backwards.* I came across it in a Fourth Avenue bookshop as a fifteen-year old sophomore who had only read Charles Baudelaire and Emily Dickinson along with staid school assignments. Di Prima's sexy, young and passionate poems were an immediate inspiration. By the time I read *Revolutionary Letters* in 1971, I was writing poetry and part of a women's writing and consciousness group. Reading di Prima changed my life.

But *Revolutionary Letters* was much more then a poetry book, it was a call to arms, a primer on how to live and embrace the counter culture. "It Takes Courage to Say no" ("Revolutionary Letter #155") admonished the reader to say, "no to canned corn and instant mashed potatoes." Di Prima fashioned a siren song from a prescient approach to food rooted in health. Further macrobiotically-tinged survival lists are given along with reminders to save water in case of riots and "hoard matches, we aren't good at rubbing sticks together anymore." In "Revolutionary Letter #4," the poet declares, "Left to themselves people grow their hair."

Printed to commemorate the fiftieth anniversary of the original *Revolutionary Letters*, this expanded collection is as potent and precious as the first missives di Prima penned.

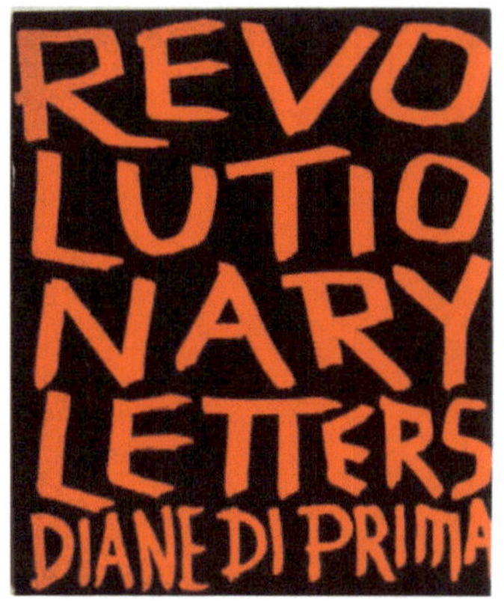

Revolutionary Letters
by Diane di Prima
City Lights Books

This current superb volume was edited by di Prima and includes more then four decades of revolutionary letters. She addresses climate change, racism, motherhood, sex, life and death with the articulate fervor that makes her one of the most significant voices of her generation.

And for further inspiration, kudos to City Lights for also publishing *Spring and Autumn Annals,* which showcases di Prima's daily writing practice as she mourned the suicide of her great friend, Fred Herko. A dancer and choreographer, his dramatic jeté from a downtown apartment ended his young life. These writings, penned to Herko, chart di Prima's grieving process and eventual healing, as she navigated a bohemian

> *... She addresses climate change, racism, motherhood, sex, life and death with the articulate fervor that makes her one of the most significant voices of her generation.*

life as a young mother and poet in the center of downtown Manhattan.

Reflective, provocative, and gossipy, di Prima navigated love affairs, published books and magazines and founded a Poet's Theater. Inclusion of archival photographs are a special addition with candid shots of a young and gorgeous di Prima, John Wieners, LeRoi Jones, and Herko. Diane di Prima embodies bohemian bravery and firsthand feminism. She remains a searing touchstone for visionary American poetry.

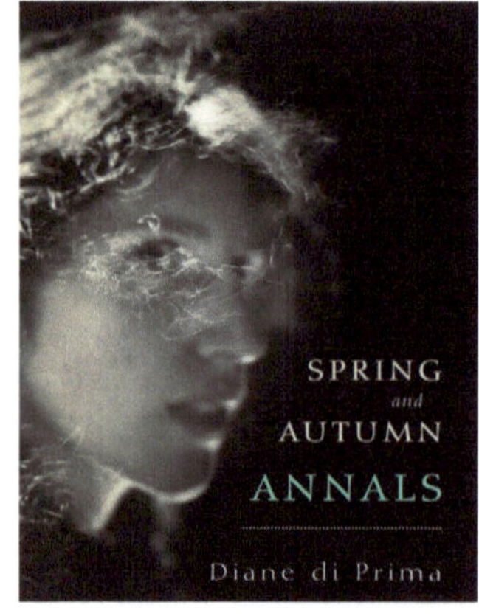

Spring and Autumn Annals
by Diane di Prima
City Lights Books

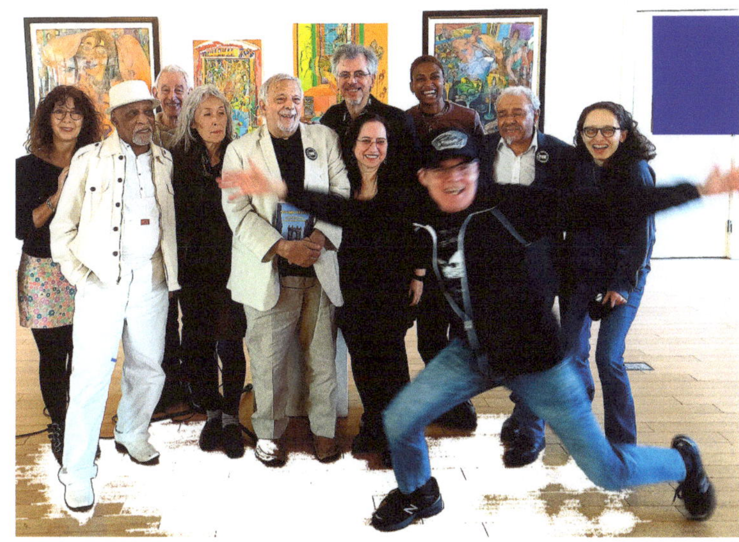

Reading at **Museo del Barrio** April 30, 2022. l to r: Christine Timm, Ngoma Hill, Angelo Verga, Yuko Otomo, George Wallace, Ewin Torres, Francine Witte, Maya Mahmud, Jesus-Papoleto Melendez, and Meagan Brothers.
Photo: E Penniman

In the name of fun and beauty, love and duty, we bring you a new *Live Mag!* .

The past year brought an anthology of New York poets from Blue Light Press. Thanks publisher **Diane Frank** and editor **George Wallace**! George hosted readings all over town including El Museo del Barrio (above). Tompkins Square librarian supremo **Alyona Glushchenkova** helped organized a reading for the tome of 189 poets at Tompkins Square Library with **John Yau, Elaine Equi**, and me.

Tompkins also hosted **Barry Wallenstein**, me, and friends **Sara Arvio, Alicia Ostriker**. We celebrated the late poet **Hillary Keel** there with **Greg Masters, Sharon Mesmer, Wanda Phipps, Lydia Cortes**—led by Associate Editor **Lori Ortiz**. Filmed by poet **Matt Proctor** (who's hosting a hot series at KGB). "Oh, Hillary … your parties were the best."

Alyona helped produce a biopic about me for NYPL! Humorous and historic, *Cuckoo O'Clock*, was directed by **Luigi Cazzaniga**.

The Café Review came out with a NYC themed issue too. **Anne Waldman, Ed Sanders, Ron Kolm,** including the late **Bernadette Mayer** and art by the late **Michael Rothenberg**. Plus art by **Trevor Winkfield, Donna Dennis**, and more. Hats off to publisher **Steve Luttrell**!

Also at El Museo del Barrio, the ambassador of Destructionist art **Rafael Montanez Ortiz**, had a monumental retrospective which I reviewed for *ArtNexus*.

We celebrated *Live* at Howl with **Andrei Codrescu, Adeena Karasick**, and photographer **Gail Thatcher**. Always grateful for Howl openings where we see friends like **Scooter LaForge, Al Diaz** and the grafitti all stars, **Brett DiPalma, Marc Miller**, and **Christy Rupp**. Deputy Edtor **Ilka Scobie** celebrated her new book at Howl. Ilka and I also read wtih **Bob Holman, Eileen Myles** and art critic **David Rimanelli** at **Arden Wohl**'s ongoing super series at Tibet House.

Maintenant mag hosted readings in tandem with their mag launch: **Lynnea Villanova, Heidi Hatry, Jane LeCroy** et al wowed the crowds at Jefferson Market Library (congrats to Librarian **Corinne Nealy** who is back after renovations). Thanks to the supreme team of **Peter Carlaftes** and **Kat Georges** of Three Rooms Press.

Our sold out launch party for issue #18 at La Mama's Poetry Electric series included artists **Judy Simonian, Moses Ros**, artist and poet **Basil King**, plus **Amber Atiya, Gregory Crosby**, and choreographer **Yoshiko Chuma**. Thanks host **William Electric Black**!

While snow fell I hung out with St. Paul resident and poet maven **Wang Ping**. We read Chinese poems for hours and even wrote one! The esteemed editors of *Rain Taxi,* **Eric Lorber** and **Kelly Everding**, took a breather to chew the literary fat with me. (We toasted our late mutual friend and publisher of *Coffee House Press*, **Allan Kornblum**).

It was nice to be invited to speak at the Poetry Project Newsletter's 50th anniversary, thanks to current editor, the gracious **Kay Gabriel** and director **Kyle Dacayun**. My fab guests were **Atanasio Di Felice, Victor Bokris, Stephen DiLauro, Barbara Rosenthal** and **Marcia Resnick**. I'd just seen Marcia's show at the Minneapolis Institute of Art. What a power! And may the power be with you.

—*JCW, February, 2023*

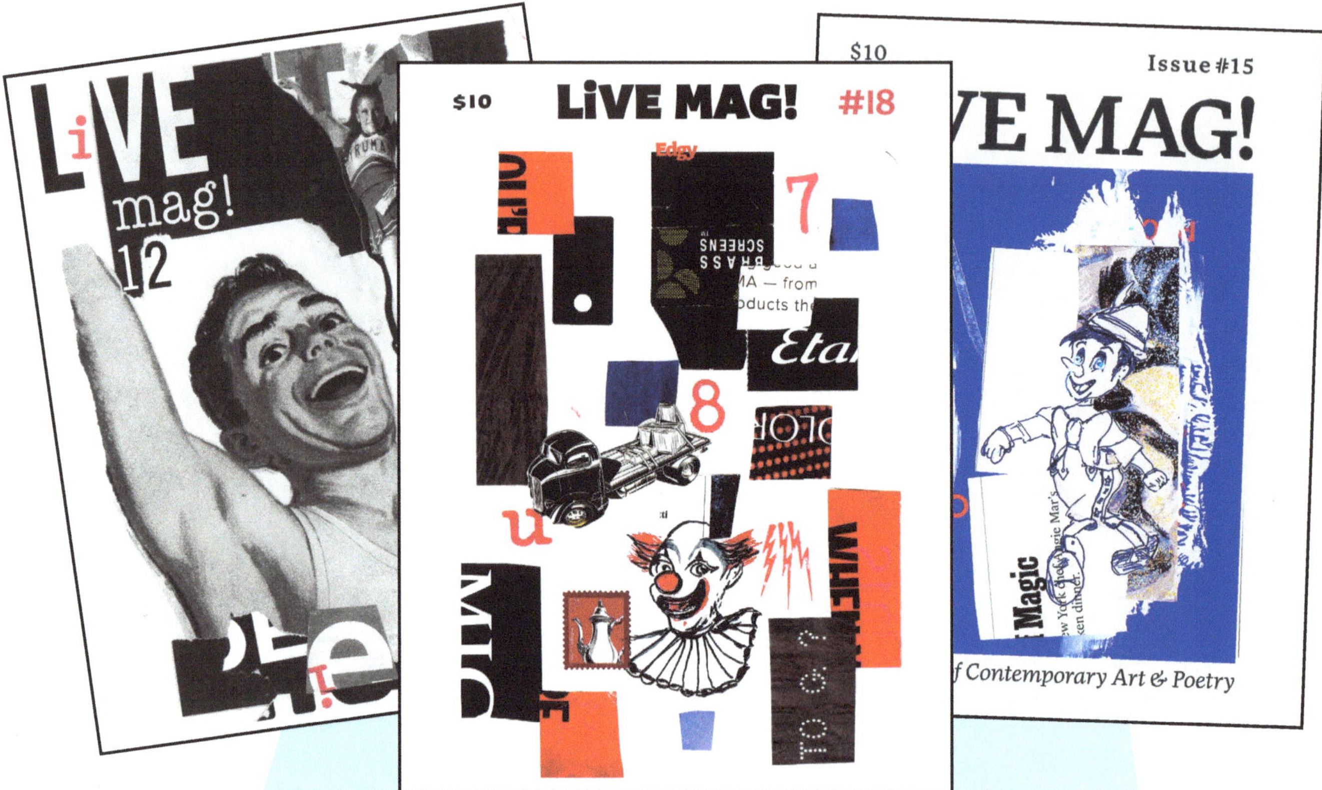

LiVE MAG!

From the stage to the page, from the wall to
the journal—each exciting issue is filled with
contemporary art and poetry. Snazzy, snappy,
and savvy—order a copy of Live! TODAY!

Small editions and rare back issues with hand-embellished covers .
Order directly from Live!
Issues also available from Ingram/Spark.

https://store.livemag.org